HOW TO BE LESS SH*T

A ROADMAP TO BEING
UNBREAKABLE
WHEN LIFE GETS TOUGH

SIMON GWILLIAM

FOREWORD BY SARAH SMITH

COPYRIGHT

Title: **How To Be Less Sh*t**
A roadmap to being unbreakable when life gets tough

Copyright © 2023 Simon Gwilliam

First published in 2023

ISBN: 9798396802520 (Paperback)

Editor: Hania Nevill

Typesetting: Colette Mason

Version: 0923-1

For everyone out there who wants more out of life but doesn't know where to start or how to keep going.

You're not flawed, you just need the right path.

You've got this.

CONTENTS

FOREWORD

Hi, It's Sarah here. I have been working alongside my good friend Simon Gwilliam for many years now, and we spent huge amounts of time developing and writing this book together (...so he suggested I write this bit, too.) Before I tell you more about him, let's say before I met him, I would have said I was not into personal development at all — with good reason, I thought!

My earlier impressions of the 'personal development' world as being filled either with overenthusiastic types (usually ex-army or ex-fitness industry) whooping and hollering about seizing the day or the nauseatingly saccharine 'Live, Laugh Love' crew weren't too far off. Still, I didn't allow room for the fact that there is a universal and innate desire in everyone to progress and to find purpose, meaning and order in a seemingly chaotic world. In this, I conceded, we are all involved in our own personal development.

I am not a religious person but I am fascinated by religion. I completed a degree in theology many years ago, and I realise now that it was people's practices for getting through life that intrigued me and drove that learning. This shared interest in people's 'methods for managing life' and putting the world to rights led me to work alongside Simon within Unbreakable. For the past few years, I have been helping him run the practical side of things, along with exploring ideas for his courses and now shaping the bones and some of the flesh of this book.

The idea, that we both passionately agreed on, is that now, more than ever, many people feel lost, overwhelmed, burned out and just don't know what to do to get out of that. There is information everywhere, and it is anxiety-inducing just trying to work out what to do or where to start.

What I like about Simon and his coaching is that you can tell he has ridden a similar roller-coaster. He's been there and done it, been lost, tried things, failed and tried again. He has been tenacious in his research. This book is the product of thousands of hours spent training people, hundreds of hours of training himself and the advice and counsel of many fascinating and wise individuals.

We feel at our worst when things don't make sense, when we feel we have little or no control, and when we are just plain exhausted.

It became clear that a step-by-step guide was needed to help people shift things ever so slightly each day until they felt a little less overwhelmed today than they did yesterday: no gimmicks, no huge goals, no huge goals, just simple steps. No telling people to 'just seize the day' or to simply 'Live, Laugh and Love'. Wonderful in intention; however, without action those words are only good for fridge magnets.

The overriding message in this book is: Life will Life you, Sh*t will happen, you will mess up, and at times you will end up feeling a bit (or a lot) rubbish. You may feel stuck or lost, or maybe you just want a bit 'more' but you are not sure what that 'more' is. Simon will guide you through the journey to be less sh*t with stories of his own in his usual straightforward and relatable style. He will teach you techniques on getting clear on what you want, mustering the energy to do something about it and then getting focussed on keeping on keeping on.

It will be your handbook for life. I sh*t you not.

ACKNOWLEDGEMENTS

There is a whole host of people who if our paths hadn't crossed, my life would have been very different.

To all my mentors throughout my life, thank you for your guidance and inspiration.

To all the great creators, such as Jesse Elder, Carl Jung, Aristotle, Marcus Aurelius, Steven Koetler, Jamie Wheal, Wim Hoff, James Nester, Garret J White, Debbie Ford, The Flow Research Collective, The Flow Genome Project, Arjuna Aishaya, Joe Dispenza, The HeartMath Institute, Dandapani and countless more: thank you for your work which has influenced Unbreakable and myself and is often referenced throughout this book.

And, of course, the members of Unbreakable itself, past and present, you are forever a source of inspiration.

INTRODUCTION

About the author

Hi, I'm Simon Gwilliam the creator of the Unbreakable Mind program. After a difficult time in my 20s, feeling lost and fighting a losing battle with my own anxiety and mind, I went on a relentless exploration of the personal development world. I transformed my own life, moving from burnt out and stuck to building a life. Since then, the Unbreakable Mind Training courses I created have helped thousands of people end their struggles and start to get the best out of their lives. I live in Malvern, Worcestershire, with my family and can often be seen walking the Malvern Hills with Milo, my chief advisor. I have a love of music, play the piano and enjoy a decent Pale Ale.

Who this book is for

Are you tired of waking up in the same old groundhog day and thinking there must be more to life? Are you continually stressed, anxious, burnt out and feel like you have nothing left to give? Do you get overwhelmed by all the information out there telling you what you should do and then struggle to get started or keep going? If so, and you want more out of your life, if you want to remove your chronic stress and anxiety, restore your energy and motivation and start living, then this book will help you do just that. Here I will show you a step-by-step, easy-to-follow path that will take the confusion and overwhelm away, enabling you to make it happen.

What this book covers

If you beat yourself up consistently, find yourself striving for perfection, falling short and in a constant stop-start cycle when making changes, then Chapter 1 will share with you a better way to approach change. Use this approach if you want to keep going and make that change stick.

Chapter 2 will help you get your spark back, overcome your fear of failure, get you clear on where you are going and remove that sense of being 'stuck' which leaves you feeling lost and powerless.

Of course, life always involves being around and dealing with other people. Chapter 3 will help you connect in a more positive way with the other people in your life and help you deal with the critical and negative influences around you, without too much conflict.

If you would like more energy and to generally feel better, Chapters 4 and 5 will be big ones for you. You will learn how to restore your energy and, more importantly, protect it so you can remain in charge of your thoughts and feelings.

Are you tired of fighting your mind? Do you want better focus and happier thoughts? Then Chapters 6 and 7 will help you understand how your mind works. More importantly, they will give you the insights and skills to go from battling your mind to making friends with it.

Finally, Chapter 8 will encourage you to take action. So, if you ever procrastinate or find you are talking yourself out of doing the things you know you want to, you will learn some practical ways to overcome that and get going.

How to get the best out of this book

Getting the most out of this book is pretty simple. The chapters are laid out step-by-step, and are designed to be read through in order. At the start of the book is a quiz. Scan the QR code (or visit www.bit.ly/htbls-quiz) to get the questions. *Take this first as it will show you where your biggest blockers to making change are.* The quiz results will show you which chapters will bring the most benefit to your situation. Of course, nothing changes without some practical action, so at the end of each chapter is a 'try this' section with simple skills to practice. (Have a pen and paper to hand to get the most out of the exercises.) After a first read, it is great to go back to things you feel stuck on. Pick up at the start of a chapter, and practise the skills laid out for you.

Keep in touch

As you use these tools, I would love it if you kept in touch and tell me how things are going. There's lots of ways to contact me and you'll find those at the end of the book. If you'd like to join our community there's information about that too.

Let's get going!

Now you know where you're heading, let's make a start on restoring your energy, removing your chronic stress and get you feeling Unbreakable. And, like planning any journey, you need to know your starting point... It's time for the quiz!

TAKE THE QUIZ

To take the quiz, simply scan the QR code with your phone's camera (or visit bit.ly/htbls-quiz).

The quiz will open up and in three minutes you will identify your biggest blocker to getting unstuck, so you can get the best out of this book. Not only that, you will receive a free video training on that exact blocker.

It's time to get cracking!

PART 1

See Greater...

1

BE LESS SH*T

Around ten years ago I was a mess. Hey, who am I kidding? At times I was a lot of a mess. I no longer knew where I was going or who I was. My anxiety was through the roof, and I felt stressed, angry, reactive, insecure and frustrated pretty much all of the time. I wanted better for my life and had no idea how to go about it. I read every book you could imagine, watched all the right YouTube videos, and followed all the popular people, yet I couldn't seem to make things stick. I couldn't seem to keep going and create the life I wanted.

I often look back and think of what advice I would give that version of me. What would I say to him to help him? I gave myself such a hard time. Constantly beating myself up for not being able to sort myself out, always looking at others, finding myself lacking in some way, and telling myself I wasn't motivated enough after each failed attempt. The thing is though, I was as motivated to seek better as you are. I was simply using so many poor methods and holding myself to such ridiculously high standards and expectations that I would always find myself lacking. I knew I wanted to change; I just couldn't make it happen. The reality was I needed a better way to do it. I needed to give myself a break while at the same time taking some responsibility for where I was.

I just needed to *'Be Less Shit.'*

Change requires us to be greater than our current reality. We must be able to see, act, feel and think slightly greater to start seeing changes. After all, nothing changes if we don't make changes. The trouble is, very often we confuse being greater with being our greatest. We are bombarded with such messages as 'Be the Best You', 'Dream Big' and 'Take Massive Inspired Action'. And surely that's what you need to hear when you are stuck in a rut? But my experience was all that over-the-top hype simply made me feel worse. It kept me in a loop where I was convinced that to move forward in life, I would have to take huge daily, inspirational actions, and if I didn't... well then, I was a failure.

The reality is *you don't have to be perfect to make progress.* You don't have to wake up every day and be the best you, bouncing through your life with every thought you have a positive one and every action you take the best possible. That pressure is not only unrealistic; in many cases, it is causing you to live in your head more, increasing your anxiety and draining your energy. This is ultimately causing you to keep stopping and giving up on yourself. You may, in fact, benefit from aiming to simply be a bit less shit.

Being less shit isn't a call for you to buck up and get on with it. It isn't saying you *are* shit. What it's saying is for you to feel better and move forward, as all you need to aim for is to be a little less shit than you currently are. Aim to do a little less of what you know doesn't help you. You don't have to go from being all over the place to living the cleanest life possible, just as you don't have to get it right and be perfect all the time. No one does.

It's a call to arms if you feel stuck looking at the huge task in front of you, wondering how you'll ever get started and if there is any point in getting started by being a little less shit today.

If you have wandered off the path of late, it's a chance to hit reset, wipe the slate clean, give yourself a break and remember that you can end the day in a slightly less shit way than you started it and get on the path to progress again.

If you look through your social media feed filled with the constant calls to live your best life while secretly beating yourself up for not being able to do it, then this is an opportunity to try something a little simpler and start moving forwards by living a slightly less shit life today.

It's a nudge if you find yourself going through a tough time or a painful time, that it can get better, that it will ease, that it will get less shit over time until it gets better. To do that, you don't need to turn it around today, you can have a less shit day today and be doing alright.

It's a reminder that if you feel a little less shit than you have done, then you are making progress. If you stack that up over time, you will eventually be in a position where you are no longer stuck, lost and confused about who you are and where you are going.

All in all, the message here is simple: Are you trying to feel better? Do you, like so many others, simply want less stress and anxiety, and more energy and enthusiasm? If you want to live a life that you are truly happy with and you are tired of constantly putting yourself under relentless pressure to always be getting it right, then I'm telling you that you don't have to be perfect to make progress. You can just aim for less shit; and as that lessens, in time you will find yourself in a completely different place from where you started.

You'll get it all wrong and that'll help you get it right

Einstein said, 'Failure is success in progress.' He also said, 'I have tried 99 times and have failed, but on the 100th time came success.' Now that's not an exact science – that every 100th attempt is the magic number. If he lived today, Albert would probably be selling his Miracle 100 Course for thousands of pounds. You may start and fail more times than that. It doesn't matter. The key is that you will get it wrong: we all balls up. Everyone is a bit shit at times. That is OK. In fact, it's all part of getting it right.

When I was younger my family had loads of interesting people call over to our house. Pete Overend Watts was one of them. He was the bass player in Mott the Hoople, a 70's rock band, and they had a fair few hits, one of them being 'All The Young Dudes', written by David Bowie. Pete used to call over a lot for cups of tea and as many biscuits as you could imagine. He was what you might call a quirky bloke, and at 16 I used to love chatting with him. He looked like a rock star/ hippy, yet he did things like walk from Land's End to John O'Groats and yet wrote a book titled The Man Who Hated Walking. He promised to release an album before he died; the main song was to be called, 'She's Real Gone'. When he found out he was dying himself, he changed the album title to, 'He's Real Gone' and organised to have it released after his death. He was an interesting man, for sure.

We were chatting one night about music and touring America, and he said that the band had split up before they had their first big hit. They didn't feel like they were getting anywhere, and it was David Bowie, who when he heard this, couldn't believe it. So, he gave them a song: All the Young Dudes. Obviously, the song was a hit, and they went on to great things.

So, what have Pete, (an old rock star) and Albert Einstein, (possibly one of the greatest scientists to ever live) got to do with you? Simple – anyone who goes on to be great at something also fails multiple times. They have all hit the point where they felt like they were wasting their time and wanted to give up on whatever it was they had set out to achieve. You will be no different. You will get it wrong, you will make mistakes, and you will definitely feel like you are getting nowhere. Making progress and feeling better won't come down to making zero mistakes and never falling off the wagon. Making progress will come down to making mistakes and keeping on going, falling off the wagon and then getting back on it again a little less slowly than before, failing forwards. I always tell people coming through our Unbreakable courses that progress is defined by how much better you are, when getting it wrong, at jumping back on and recovering. Unfortunately, so many tend to think that success will come from always getting things right. From here on, drop that belief and aim to get better at getting it wrong and recovering after. Let's finish with some words of wisdom from Overend himself.

"Simo, you should be a frontman in a band; you have the personality for it..."

"But I can't sing, Pete?"

"Don't worry about it. None of the good ones can!"

Maybe he was exaggerating, or maybe he had a point. It's easy for you to think that if you are to make changes, you need to get things right all the time and that you need to be great at everything from the off. That you can't start something because everything isn't perfect, or the time isn't right. Just start!

You will get things wrong on your journey. Sometimes, you will find it hard and fall off the wagon. It's part of the process. Remember, stop beating yourself up and get back to it because we must all start somewhere.

Shit happens

Life has a way of showing up with stuff for you to deal with. Shit really does happen. Life really does life you, and at times there is absolutely nothing you can do about it except hold on for the ride and stay in the game.

Like you, life hasn't always felt fair or kind to me. We live in a world where many believe that the universe always rewards good people and that good things will happen if you are a good person. The trouble is that life doesn't always work that way, and very often, bad things happen to good people, and when you believe that life is always giving you what you deserve, you can start to feel betrayed. The fact of the matter is bad things happen to good people. Shit does happen, and at times, all you can do is pick yourself up, give yourself a break and allow yourself to be where you are and just try to feel slightly less shit each day.

No one is immune to pain. Many people will tell you that 'no one can make you feel anything', but I disagree. I used to say that too, yet it was more in hope than belief. It was more a shield to try and hide behind in desperation than a principle in which I could honestly believe. Life *does* make you feel things. Your power and strength and progress will come after that. It will come in what you do next, in how you process and deal with the shitty stuff, and that's tough. We all know the pain and frustration that comes with rejection, loss and failure; the hurt that comes with that, the horrible heavy feeling in the heart, the emotions that seem like they will never leave – the frustration at being unable to move them on. Life is so much out of our control, and bad things do happen. Bad things happen to good people all the time.

I'd say a considerable amount of people join Unbreakable because something has happened; something or someone has knocked them sideways. A lady in our academy shared this the other day:

> "I remember when I started 'Unbreakable,' I asked Simon, 'Do you really think I can turn my life around?'"
>
> "He responded, 'Do you think you can turn your life around?'"
>
> "I replied, 'Yes, I think so.' ...and I have."

When you hear that the lady in question had lost two young children at different points in her life, amongst other things, you can see why she asked the question. Was the journey smooth? Far from it. Very often, it was one step forward and two steps back. There were setbacks and tough times, yet she moved forward with things getting a little less shit as time went on, and there she was, in her own words, "life turned around".

Do the feelings associated with the 'bad shit' ever go away? No, of course not. I know that for many of you dealing with the stuff life throws at you, the thought of making things overly positive doesn't wash. You've been to the puppet show and seen the strings. You may need a different aim to get you going. A different hope. A hope that things can be slightly less shit until they can start to get much better.

The 'most dangerous' time to be alive

Many military scholars agree that the battlegrounds of World War I were the most treacherous and deadly in modern warfare because it was there that modern weapons met mediaeval methods of engagement. I don't know how true that is or how you can even quantify something like that, but what got me intrigued was:

> "When modern weapons met mediaeval methods."

This rings true for modern life: we are at an unprecedented time in our evolution. Our technological advancements are accelerating at a rate far greater than the physical and mental methods we have to cope with them. My Dad's life at my age was much smaller than mine is. It was much more local; he only knew what was going on in his life, his job and the lives of the people he knew. The news was in bitesize bulletins and not available 24/7. He listened to the headlines, grumbled and got about his day. In a nutshell, the internet and 24hr TV channels have connected us to a bigger, faster, more opinionated world, and so has social media. Yet here we are, working with mediaeval methods and systems to handle all this exposure and using outdated philosophies and skills to help us navigate it all. That is why, in my opinion, life can be a dangerous war zone for many. You only have to look at the mental health statistics that have been published recently to see that something is up:

> In any given week in England, six in 100 people will be diagnosed with a generalised anxiety disorder.
>
> (Source: Mind)
>
> In the UK, over eight million people are experiencing an anxiety disorder at any one time.
>
> (Mental Health UK)
>
> 88% of UK employees have experienced at least some level of burnout over the last two years.
>
> (HR News UK)
>
> Although the suicide rate in the UK has declined across the population over the last 40 years, the suicide rate among men has increased and is three times more likely in men than in women.
>
> (Samaritans)

A few hundred years ago, the printing press revolutionised the transmission of information among the population and ultimately had a large part to play in revolutions and a renaissance in thinking across Europe. Moving forward a few years, radio and subsequently television could be called the great democratisers of society. For example, the introduction of television allowed people, who wouldn't typically have had the means, to watch an opera, a Shakespeare play or politicians in action. A free flow of information began, and opinions were generated. There is no doubt that people who were once overlooked could begin to have a say and society had to catch up. Ways of thinking had to evolve. Today, we can all recognise that the leap forward in communication and access to information has been tremendous, and it has happened with a rapidity that makes the eyes water.

People can argue that information and options to help ourselves are everywhere now, so, it should be easier than ever to get ourselves together and move forwards. Yet all this information has an opposite and overwhelming effect. The more choices you have, the harder it becomes to choose. The more ways you can find to help yourself, the more confused you become. *The more confused you become, the less action you take.* All that information adds more stress to your life, which is undoubtedly stressful and busy enough. More overwhelming information is the last thing you need. Modern skills delivered at the right time and in the most user-friendly order will help you make changes in day-to-day life. You need a new modern way of doing things that removes the overwhelm that comes with change, not adds to it.

I get it. At the start of my journey, I was searching for an answer and trying everything by reading all the books then trying to figure out what to do with the information. Joining membership sites and never going through the vast back catalogue of information videos. Always following everything and everyone on Facebook, watching YouTube videos and getting all hyped up to change things but not knowing how to. Downloading all the apps for breathing, meditation and accountability, yet getting bored with them and doubting that they were working. Add to that, setting and resetting goals every five minutes, and it was a perfect storm for causing more chaos than was being removed. Nothing was changing, and what did change didn't seem to last. If anything, stress and overwhelm were getting worse rather than better. After yet another failed attempt a realisation hit me – all I had been doing was learning, but I had very few practical skills to put into action and certainly no plan. There is no step-by-step, simple path to follow that guarantees results. I looked everywhere and there was nothing to follow laid out for me, just information and more information. That was the birth of Unbreakable Mind Skills, right there. The step-by-step practical skills plan came into being.

Don't get me wrong; it's changed a whole lot since the first version all those years ago. Now we have the Unbreakable Path: a 12-month step-by-step skills course that functions much like a game, moving up levels as you progress, winning awards for milestones and taking upgrades to help you get better at certain things. In fact, based on data gathered from previous clients, over 12 months gave some impressive results for changes in the average person's daily wellbeing.

Increases

Motivation+200%

Happiness +196%

Clarity on life+260%

Reductions

Stress   -84%

Overwhelm -79%

Anxiety   -84%

So, what am I saying? I am saying two things.

The secret to getting unstuck and really changing your life isn't getting it all perfect and never failing, nor is it a case of being bombarded with more information and stuff you 'should' do while trying to think positively. It's being given the right skill at the right time, with an emphasis on being less shit as you go: that's the Unbreakable recipe for success, and that's the way that this book will break it all down for you.

It's not your fault that you have found it so hard to make changes stick. We are living in modern times using mediaeval methods. We are overwhelmed with information, more aware than ever before but trying to use the same old, outdated skills, and it's time to address that.

Try this

Have a go at this simple exercise and reflect on how your need to get everything perfect has affected your results in life. Also, consider where you have previously been successful despite not always getting it right. Awareness of how this has played out in your life is crucial to helping you make changes. You will need a pen and paper and nothing more.

Step 1: Reflect on your previous imperfect success

A. Write down an achievement in your life. Something you made happen. This can be anything, professional or personal: raising kids, passing an exam, buying a house...

_____

_____

_____

B. Think back to the start. What obstacles and setbacks did you have to overcome to achieve it?

_____

_____

_____

_____

_____

_____

_____

_____

_____

C. Think over the journey. Note how it could have been better, but you still managed to achieve what you set out to do.

_____

_____

_____

_____

_____

_____

_____

_____

_____

A quick recap

Change requires you to be greater, not your greatest. Being less shit as an aim will help you remember that and put less pressure on yourself.

You don't need to be perfect to make progress in your life.

1. You will get it wrong and fail at things, but it doesn't mean you will never make the changes you want. Failing is part of the process, not a sign that you're doing badly and should quit.

2. Bad things happen to good people. Life at some point lifes everyone. Understanding that it's not personal and that you aren't flawed in some fundamental way will help you navigate this. We all have to deal with what life throws at us, at some point.

3. The world is changing, and your skills are outdated. You need modern skills to deal with life and thrive. It's not your fault you don't have the right skills; no one teaches them.

2

DON'T LET YOUR SPARK GO OUT

I love this beauty of a paragraph by Ayn Rand. It describes the battle we can experience to break free of where we are in order to move onto something better, and how often we can allow our spark to die out setback by setback, until we convince ourselves that we don't want better at all.

> "Do not let your fire go out, spark by irreplaceable spark in the hopeless swamps of the not-quite, the not-yet, and the not-at-all. Do not let the hero in your soul perish in lonely frustration for the life you deserved and have never been able to reach. The world you desire can be won."
>
> Ayn Rand

But it's OK to want better for yourself, your life and the people around you. Sometimes, it's drilled into people just to be grateful or content – of course, these are both great aims. The thing is, why does it have to be either/or? Why can't you be happy and content with your life and still pursue a little better? For many, that simply becomes a little excuse, so you don't have to face up to the fact that you would like 'different.' You think if you just stop wanting, then the pain of not being able to get there will go away. Yet it doesn't. It remains in all the constant daily reminders around you. It's understandable; life can be challenging. You try, you fail, you get knocked back, and as the beautiful passage above says; very often you can let the 'hero in your soul perish with lonely frustration'. However, 'The world you desire can be won.'

Jung said:

> "People will do anything, no matter how absurd, in order to avoid facing their own soul."

How true is that when it comes to avoiding admitting what we want out of life? We do all sorts of absurd things. We lie to ourselves and others about what we truly want, we sedate ourselves with mindless activities and vices to numb the desire for more, and we even use positive thinking about the life we have as a form of denial. All this just so we can stay where we are. Yet deep down, we know there is better or different or more for us.

That pull to be a little more of some things and a little less of others – that's *you*. That's the real you calling you to make changes and to be more you. You can deny it for so long, but eventually, you will get kick-back and your soul will tell you that this isn't what you want. It lets you know that there has to be more to life than this, and there is that choice again. Do you hide away from that, or do you allow yourself to see a bit greater? Do you let yourself look beyond your current life to what could be a brighter future? Change becomes impossible if you cannot be honest about the changes you would like to make. Progress never happens if you don't know the progress you would like to see, and so each time you deny it, your spark burns out just a touch more.

But I don't know what I want

Is it that you don't know what you want or have you become good at pretending you don't know what you want? Or, perhaps, that you are just really good at refusing to acknowledge what you want at all, for that acknowledgement may open you up to the pain of not having it? I would ask you this; are you even more guilty of focusing on what you don't want in life? What you believe has gone wrong, what is irritating you, what you have lost, what you regret and what you plain old hate about your life. We are all very good at studying our pain. This snippet of Bruce Springsteen's Thunder Road hits the nail on the head perfectly:

> "You can hide 'neath your covers and study your pain
> Make crosses from your lovers, throw roses in the rain
> Waste your summer praying in vain for a saviour to rise
> from these streets"

You've been there — we all have — hiding beneath the covers (whatever you use as covers), studying your pain. Maybe life 'lifed' you. Maybe you lost something or someone or somewhere, or perhaps there has just been a build-up over time of the same old crap until you have no idea how you ended up where you are. It's a horrible experience to be sat feeling that pain, that kind of discomfort, the never-ending feeling in your chest, the sadness or the hurt or whatever it is for you. It's even harder when you lose hope that it will ever leave you.

That, for me, is when people give up. They give up on what they want and make do with what is.

Studying your pain will only get you so far, like picking at a scab, this constant attention to our discomfort seems to keep it hanging around. However, there is a glimmer of light because lying buried within the pain of what you no longer truly want are the seeds of your desire. The path to who you are is hidden amongst all that pain and frustration.

To access that, though, you have to do something none of us wants to do, which is to be completely honest, radically honest, about where you are. You have to admit to yourself that deep down, you want more. You have to admit that. You have to face up to the discomfort of saying that this isn't what you want for your life and at the same time, understand that it's OK. You will stumble, fall and end up in places where you don't want to end up. That's not failure. If anything, failure is pretending you don't care and that is where the responsibility chat comes in. Being honest with yourself and taking responsibility for what you aren't happy with in your life doesn't mean you are at fault. It doesn't mean that all of your life's problems are now your doing. Maybe some aren't. As you well know, life can beat all of us up even when we have done nothing to encourage that.

Even though things may not be your fault, it's always up to you to decide what happens next and doing that with some compassion is critical. It's easy to shame yourself and say that you are a failure because you failed at something, to say that you are rubbish because life is going rubbish. ***Shame doesn't help you move forward.*** If anything, feeling shame and guilt keeps you stuck right where you are as well as being defined by your life as it is. In my experience, the more honest you are about where you are and what you don't want, the clearer you will be on what you *do* want. After all, if you are complaining about your life with great energy, then what you want is totally in the opposite direction. Whatever you are honest about not wanting anymore is a signpost towards what you do want. Don't like your job? What don't you like about it? What is the opposite of that? Fed up of feeling crap? How do you honestly feel? What does that stop you from doing? What does it make you do that you'd rather not? What's the opposite of that? You get the picture. The only time in life I have been unable to help someone get clear on what they would like next in life is when they aren't willing to be truly honest and accept responsibility for where they are right now.

Eventually, you will want to look forward to what you would like in life. Never an easy step because you have to want to take it, and sometimes you just won't want to. The potential change and effort involved may seem too big and scary, or you may feel you need to know why you are where you are. However, you don't need the answers to why you are where you are before you decide to start moving forward. You find them when you start moving forward, and in the moving forwards, little by little being less shit each day, change ceases to seem scary and becomes achievable.

Forgive yourself relentlessly

Eventually, the pull to move forward becomes so strong that you can't fail to hear it. The moment arrives when you say:

> 'Right! I need to sort this out.'

I remember that moment perfectly in my life. Sat alone in my house, which was meant to be a beautifully renovated cottage yet was still a shell with no doors, windows or even a back wall. I'd been trying to sort myself out for ages and made another right balls-up the night before which led to a phone call with my Mum telling me that my Dad was disappointed in me. (Which, looking back, took some nerve considering some of the capers he had pulled in his life.) Either way, I came off that phone call feeling rubbish, lost and confused about what to do next and there it was: 'Right... I need to sort myself out.'

It's never a comfortable feeling to realise things need to change. We all want to avoid the truth of who we are. We all have those moments when it gets too much, and we know we must face it all. Without those moments, nothing changes. Here is the kicker: the tough bit becomes letting go of who you have been so you can go and become who you really are.

I spent so long and so much energy trying not to be the version of me that kept cocking up that I had no energy left to be the one I truly wanted to be. Here's what I wish I had realised; *you don't have to punish yourself for who you have been to become better*. Oddly, possibly as a result of social conditioning (that's another book entirely), we humans can be a guilt-ridden bunch when we realise things can't go on as they are, as then we start to feel shame for who we have been and what we have done.

Shockingly, many people will encourage you to do that too; ,to shame yourself into action. Yes, you can use shame to fuel you into change, but it will catch up with you in the end, and when it does, it will hit you like a ton of bricks. You must forgive yourself for who you have been to move forward. Shame and guilt are literal killers, in many cases, and when does it end? When do your mistakes get let go of and your failures met with compassion? I'm not talking about being forgiven by anyone else; I'm talking about forgiving yourself. When do you seek a sense of compassion and understanding for those things? Maybe you feel that punishing yourself makes it better. It doesn't. What is done is done. Perhaps you think that if you carry the guilt and shame about who you have been, then this will stop you from making those mistakes again. It doesn't. It eats away at you, makes you a victim and will shape your behaviour in ways that continue not to help. As the saying goes, 'what you resist will persist.' You simply, at some point, have to say that enough is enough and forgive yourself.

Of course, this isn't an easy gig. The society you live in can play a big part in adding to your feelings of shame and guilt. They are quick to attack, critique and judge anyone who doesn't meet the exacting standards created in some odd, collective societal decision. But I'm not talking to society right now. I am talking to you. You, who has reached the point where you have punished yourself enough for who you have been and who now needs to let go so you can become who you can be. I know the world seems to hate second chances, yet when it comes to yourself, I encourage you to **give yourself all the opportunities you need to learn, start again and attempt to do better.**

At this point, you may be thinking that people can't just go around thinking they can do what they like, then forgive themselves and repeat. What about the way their actions affect other people? What about *that* guilt and shame? You're right. I'm not saying you can just go about wreaking havoc and face no consequences, because that is pure indulgence. That's someone indulging in their mistakes, repeating them and not learning from them. Forgiving yourself means that you'll have already been beating yourself up. If your actions have affected other people, you will already know the pain, shame, and guilt of that, and by forgiving yourself, you have met it head-on, learnt from it and decided you will do better next time.

Forgiving yourself is about looking forward, without beating yourself up for an extended period about what has passed. It is recognising your mistakes and making the necessary adjustments to improve as you move forward.

You honour the pain you may have caused rather than indulge it. How does it help anyone if you to wallow in the pain that you have caused other people? If anything, doing that makes it all even more about you. It is a form of irritating self-indulgence.

Carrying around guilt and shame for who you have been helps no one, not even the people affected by your actions. When I think of the young man who had that 'right!' moment, sitting alone in that shell of a house, I no longer feel guilt and shame for who I was. I feel compassion for him. I can see I was simply doing the best I could with what I had at the time, and now I know better and can do better. The same goes for you. You are, and have been, doing your best with what you have. Now that you have had that 'right!' moment, don't turn your back on who you have been and shame and guilt yourself. Now that you are more self-aware and can see better, let go and forgive yourself. Noticing how that shows up in your life is a great place to start.

How do you behave when you are shaming yourself? What behaviours show up in your day-to-day life when you are holding on to past mistakes and who you have been? What does it cause you to do? What does it stop you from doing? Notice and ask yourself what behaviours you could replace those with. It may sound too simplistic to approach it that way, however, the more you break those habits bit by bit, the more you can stop repeating the past and start creating your future.

Avoiding failure makes you feel like one

You will have many reasons for not creating the life you want if you are truly honest, though deep down, it's usually related to fear. When you hear people talk about fear in self-help work, it's always dramatic, but in my experience, fear is sneaky. It's always trying to infiltrate your thinking, coming in under the radar using tactics like logic and positive thinking, so it doesn't sound like fear at all. In fact, it sounds very practical.

It sounds like:

> 'It's not the right time, I just need to wait until...'

Or positives like:

> 'maybe things aren't so bad, life could be worse...'

... and that's because in order not to feel the fear you tell a nice little story about it, so you can avoid feeling it altogether. The trouble is that it keeps you stuck. It takes you back to where you just tried to come from.

Don't beat yourself up for that. We all feel fear, and we have all been, in some way, conditioned to avoid feeling it at all. The saying, 'there is nothing to fear about fear, except fear itself,' is pretty valid. Humans fear feeling afraid, much as they fear a lot of feelings. That's because you have felt afraid, and someone with good intentions tried to stop you from feeling that way and bang! You now view fear as being a bad thing.

Yet fear is fuel. Fear is energy, which when harnessed and directed towards what you want can help you. When suppressed and avoided, fear keeps you stuck. So, what are you afraid of? Failure, rejection, looking stupid, and not being enough are all big players in the fear stakes, but you often don't recognise your fear as having its roots in those things. The person who, deep down, wants a relationship rarely says:

> "I cancelled that blind date because I am afraid of feeling rejected."

Instead, it's always something like:

> "I don't need someone anyway..."

Or:

> "I realised I am OK on my own..."

...before going back to wondering if they will ever meet the right person. Those of you who want to leave your job rarely say:

> "I didn't apply for that perfect one I saw because I am afraid of failing".

You say things like "at least my job is safe right now" or "better the devil you know than the devil you don't" before returning to the daily grind long enough to contemplate leaving again.

The person who's felt the pull of getting in shape doesn't say they avoided their gym induction because they were afraid of looking stupid. They say things like "it's not the right time at the minute" or "I'll start next month" knowing full well they won't until they catch a glimpse of their reflection and decide they really do need to do something... (again.)

We all do this. Everyone on the planet does this. Even all those self-help people that you follow. There is nothing wrong with you because you try to talk yourself out of things. Nothing is broken about you because you allow fear to get the better of you and make the most random justifications. Deep down, most of us fear not being enough: not good enough, not smart enough, not attractive enough, not funny enough. Deep down, you believe you have to be more of 'something' to be happy, successful or accepted, and if you reach outside of what you currently do you will be found out. You will be found not to be enough.

Think how often you have avoided doing something you really wanted or that you know would have been good for you and used logic to justify not doing it. If you search your feelings, you know that deep down, for the most part, you were avoiding it through fear.

However, the reality, that I have seen play out over and over again, is that when you start to notice the little stories that keep you stuck, you decide to move forwards anyway. You see that you really are enough to make it work and you always have enough of whatever is required. Nothing keeps your spark alive more than moving through the irrational fears you have about yourself and towards what you truly want.

Find out what you do, and then stop doing it

As much as fear stops us from getting started, some things stop us from keeping going. After all, getting started on your vision of a better life is one thing; keeping going towards it is another. At some point, on the path to greater things all of us can get stuck and lose momentum. The 'Emotional Cycle of Change' has been done to death in the self-help industry because it makes so much sense.

If you are unfamiliar with it, the theory of The Emotional Cycle of Change says that when you start something you are optimism personified and are pretty uninformed about what the journey ahead will be like. As you progress, you begin to get informed about the difficulties involved yet remain optimistic. As the difficulties stack up and your progress slows you hit the Valley of Despair, and it's make or break time: you can knuckle down and progress through the dip or quit and repeat the cycle. If you are consistently stuck in an area (weight loss and fitness or learning a new skill are always solid examples), you can be sure that you will repeat that cycle a great deal.

Yet why do you quit when you hit that dip? Most of you will stop because you think you are getting nowhere, which feels uncomfortable.

George Leonard wrote a great book, Mastery, which broke this down incredibly well. It was his work, in fact, that helped us shape and inform what eventually became some of our Unbreakable Principles. The fact of the matter is, whenever you set off to improve something you will hit that dreaded plateau.

That can be confusing because you are still doing the stuff that got you this far. If anything, maybe you are doing more than before, so why are you getting nowhere? Because that is how change works. When you first start anything new, you have an initial burst of progress. Then you begin to adapt and create a new normal, and being a human being there are always systems under your surface working to keep things as comfortable as possible. These systems, rooted in your psychology, neurology and your very evolution, are there to maintain inner balance and energy conservation. If something seems like hard work then your human programming generally does not like it very much, and your progress can begin to slow to a halt. At this point your mental patterns kick in, because the ironic thing is that these plateaus are uncomfortable. The plateau doesn't feel as good as the rush of progress you were making. You can feel disappointed, frustrated and even like you are failing. But you aren't failing. Plateaus are natural, and if you keep doing the work required, you will move through the plateau and experience another burst of progress, and the whole thing repeats. The trouble is that you love to avoid the plateau because you love to avoid discomfort, but by doing so you tend to live in it.

George Leonard mapped out three ways people avoid breaking through a plateau. Having seen thousands of people come through our Unbreakable Courses, I can confidently say these traits show up without fail. We use different names, but the general principles exist:

The 'Shiny Object'

You know you fall into this pattern if you get distracted by a miracle 'easier' option when you hit the plateau. This is a popular one. It's why fad diets and miracle supplements that cure your anxiety are all the rage. The promise of get-rich-quick schemes involving no work are so often attractive. The trouble is, deep down, you know that these things don't work. You want them to, but they don't, and all they do is distract you from doing the things that actually work and the progress you have made. It's an attractive way to avoid the frustrating plateau because you get to be all excited over and over again. Unfortunately, for the Shiny Object fan, you will stay going round and round on the same old merry-go-round and getting nowhere.

The Perfectionist

This pattern can be a little more destructive. You start something and are all in. You hit the plateau and decide to break through it by sheer strength of will and determination. You up the effort and obsessively double down on being even more perfect. After all, your lack of progress must be down to needing to be more perfect than you were... right? Eventually, you burn out after doing everything you can to break through and rush through this plateau. You implode, and it's usually in a big, destructive way that sends you spiralling back to where you started. Or you decide to start again and so make your way back to the beginning to try and get it all right. Cue another repeat of the same until you end up burnt out completely.

The Hacker

This pattern is a strange one; it's when you get so far and decide to just live on the plateau. The 'This Will Do' crew don't accept the plateau, but they tolerate it. They resolve to manage their anxiety and stress, tolerate their crappy job, and can often be heard saying things like "Well, that's life", "That's just the way it is", "It could be worse" or "Why rock the boat?"

It's where, in my experience, dreams go to die. In the long term, it is exhausting micro-managing and numbing one's mind and emotions enough to remain OK with being sat on the plateau for any length of time. It's exhausting and disheartening to give up and tolerate a life you don't want.

Managing the plateau

We all have these patterns, but you, me, everyone has a way of escaping the discomfort of the plateau. You have your go-to methods, and you may use all of them at different times and in various areas of your life. Your job is to notice and have a go at altering your pattern — even if just a little to start with.

So, how can you manage the plateau? Well, in Leonard's work, 'mastery' is the way to approach the plateau and we have all, believe it or not, done just that with something in our lives. We have all accomplished something in our lives with the approach that Leonard refers to as mastery. In Unbreakable, we break working with mastery down into the three P's; three things you can use to navigate the plateau with some skill and grace when you can accept and practice them.

Patience

All significant results and changes in your life will require patience: patience with the process and with yourself. You will get it wrong and you will make mistakes. You will hit the plateau and try to quit. Maybe you do quit. Notice, forgive yourself and get back in the game. Remind yourself that the plateau is normal. Every great master of their craft has previously and still does go through the plateau; they are just practising more patience than most people.

Practice

When you are on the plateau, forget your obsession with the goal and the results you want. I know the self-help industry, in general, tells you that the more you focus on the goal the faster the results will come, yet in this case, the more obsessed you become with the outcome, the further away you will feel you are getting. Instead of 'goal obsessed', become 'practice obsessed'. By that, I mean focusing on taking care of the things you are doing and doing them well. When you do that, the results take care of themselves.

Progress

Don't forget the progress you have made. It's easy to focus on where you are and want to be, yet it's much more beneficial to focus on where you are now and where you started. Not only that, but seek to measure your progress in more ways than just results. Track your habits, and give yourself credit for setbacks overcome. Progress is measured in more ways than simply the 'results' you are experiencing.

As another saying states 'find out how you will mess it all up and don't go there'. The patterns you display when trying to avoid the plateau are definitely one of the ways that you usually balls it all up. Be mindful of them, be aware of them when they show up. Give them a smile, don't beat yourself up and remind yourself that, should you find yourself 'sliding', it's just a natural way that we all try to avoid the discomforts, perceived or actual, that we are facing. Focus on being patient and practising the things that work and your progress, and you will navigate it much more smoothly.

Constantly giving up on yourself and returning to old patterns dims the spark and fire inside you. To keep going involves knowing your patterns and attempting to fall into them a little less as you go.

Try this

Grab a pen and paper. It's time to put some of the things you have been learning into practice. The following steps will help you get clear on what you want and how that could look in your life, before leaving you with a list of further steps you can start to take straight away. This is key to getting more out of your life. It's not as hard as you might think, and you can come back to these steps as often as you like in the future to help you get clear on where you're going.

Step 1: Find what you want

A. Divide a page in half and on the left-hand side write 'Don't wants' and on the right-hand side, 'Do wants'.

B. Write everything you don't want in your life in the left-hand column. Don't censor yourself. Write how you feel, what you do, what you tolerate and how daily life looks day to day.

C. Flip all the things in your 'Don't want' column to their opposite. So, if you wrote 'angry', maybe you flip that to 'calm', or 'tired' to 'energised' and note that in the right-hand column.

D. You now have a list of things you want and not just a long list of things you don't want.

Step 2: Explore how life could be

Describe how a week in this life would look and feel on paper. Use the ideas below to help you:

- What will you be doing from day to day?
- What will your weekends and time off consist of?
- How is your social life?
- How will you feel throughout your day?
- How will you feel when engaging with friends and family?
- What do your mornings look like?
- What do you find easier?
- What habits are in place?

How does your day-to-day life look now?

How do you feel before going to bed?

Step 3: Find some actions to take

A. Divide a page in half and title the left-hand side 'Stop Doing' and the right-hand side 'Start Doing'.

B. List everything you need to stop doing in order to move towards what you want.

C. Flip all the 'Stops' to their opposite and write that down in the right-hand column.

D. Pick one of the 'Starts' and do it right now.

Now you have more of an idea about what you want or how to figure out what you want. The next step is learning how to bring other Starts into all of this and how to handle the inevitable issues that crop up when you start to change things in your life.

A quick recap

Everyone gets lost and lets the fire inside go out. The key to getting it back is being radically honest with yourself about what you don't want and what you do want.

1. You cannot get unstuck and create a brighter future for yourself if you keep beating yourself up about your past. You don't have to punish yourself for who you were to become better.

2. Fear stops us from moving forward, and we often mask it with logic and justification to avoid feeling it. Notice how that shows up for you and the stories you tell so you can move past them.

3. You will plateau in your pursuit of change. The plateau is a sign you have made progress. If you stick through it, more will come.

4. Be aware of your learning style. It often shows up on the plateau and stops you from continuing to move forwards.

5. The three P's of mastery will help you make it through the plateau: practice, patience and persistence.

3

IT'S NOT ALL ABOUT YOU, YOU KNOW?

The biggest mistake I have ever made in my pursuit of a better life is the absence of considering and including other people.

At times that hurt people, at times, it hurt me, and it took me a long time to realise the error of my ways.

Personal development can be selfish, and you can spend so long focusing on yourself that you forget that there is far more to life than just you. What is the point of any of it if it doesn't improve your life inside *and* out? For yourself *and* others?

When considering your vision for life, relationships are not only a good thing to be working on, they are *vital* for your health and happiness. You may piously think, 'Well, I am always doing things for people, so I have that covered'. It's not quite as simple as that. Maybe you think that you don't need anybody in your life. It's not quite as simple as that either. There are those, with many more letters after their names than me, that would say that the Harvard Study of Adult Development is one of the most extensive studies on mental and physical health. I won't try to break the whole thing down. Here is a brief outline though:

> In study, Harvard tracked two groups of men. Beginning in the 1930s, 724 men were involved. One group were Harvard graduates (by the nature of the US College system of the time, they would have been from wealthy, highly educated, mostly white families), and one group were from Boston's poorest neighbourhoods. All the men were 19 years old when they entered the study, and in the last article I read about them, 60 were still alive and in their 90s. Everything was tracked across their lives through questionnaires, interviews with them and their families, medical records, blood samples, brain scans and more. So, what was discovered? It was concluded that good relationships are the most significant factor in how happy and healthy you will end up.

> The study found that having good social connections is one of the best markers for better health and well-being, and conversely, loneliness does in fact kill. Having higher-quality close links is more important for our well-being than the number of general connections we have, and having good relationships is good for both our bodies and brains.

When I read that study and looked across my own life, it hit me like a ton of bricks. I realised that for all of my work on myself, I had forgotten about the importance of the people I cared about. As the saying goes, the truth hurts, and it was a wake-up call to something I already knew. We humans have a wonderful way of avoiding what we know needs to be faced, because it's uncomfortable. The fact of the matter is we are all wired for connection. Some of us are hugely social, some not, but we all have a need and a desire for connection.

You will know the feeling of loneliness, and we all have an innate knowledge that loneliness is as bad for our health as alcohol or smoking, but now scientists have actually proven that. When experiencing loneliness, your health declines more quickly, your brain doesn't function well and you lose empathy for others and yourself. In rats, isolation has even been shown to increase the size of tumours. You are built and have evolved to have social connection with others. You only have to look at how often your daydreaming is about others or how much you ruminate over issues that include others and relationships. The fabric of us wants us to have solid connections with other people.

You may hear that and panic, but the key here is to remember that it is the quality of relationships that benefits us more than the quantity. You may think you need lots of social connections, yet as the Harvard study shows us, it is the quality of those connections that makes the difference. Many of us aren't comfortable with huge amounts of social activity but don't confuse that with not liking people, being introverted or socially anxious. So often people label themselves as 'socially anxious' because the 'successful' life you are sold is filled with hordes of friends, and not everyone has or wants that. Not many of us do, if truth be told. Far better to have a couple of really close and connected friends than masses of acquaintances.

Often these days, however, people don't have a meaningful connection with anyone. Very often, the quality of our relationships is simply transactional. You serve and help others all day long – kids, colleagues, customers and partners – swiftly moving from one interaction or act of service to another without any quality connection. Quality is the crucial qualifier here. High-conflict relationships are detrimental to our health, more so than not having any relationships at all, and family feuds that involve holding grudges are shown to be equally bad for us.

What is a high-quality relationship, then? Well, back to the study. It was found that high-quality relationships aren't all hunky dory each day, they still have issues, but the critical factor is that you know you can always count on the other person and guess what... that takes work, doesn't it? You can romanticise relationships, friendships and any other connections you may have, and perhaps believe the social media posts about how good relationships shouldn't need work and that they should always be easy and flow without hindrance. Still, they do have problems, and they do have bumps. You get out what you put into life, and quality relationships will undoubtedly come from quality effort.

So why do so many of us not prioritise these relationships? Another Harvard study's survey, of people leaving American colleges, cited that:

> 80% of graduates said being rich was their main priority and 50% said being famous was.

Of course. money is an important factor in life, there is no denying that. A lack of financial security is one of the most stressful things we can go through. Yet to put it above our relationships, to put our career success over our relationships is something I have truly been guilty of. Maybe we believe it's one or the other and that we can't have both. Yet if you search your feelings, you will find little evidence that this is the case. Perhaps, like all things, some people simply feel that uncomfortable resistance around connecting with others. You are a bit scared of getting hurt, rejected or let down, so to mask that feeling you tell yourself it doesn't matter. Or the other and most inexcusable reason: you just don't make time for other people in a meaningful way. You don't schedule time with your friends and forget to send that message 'just to say hi'. You let life run away with you, and before you know it, you have let your most important connections slide.

The idea that the road to success is often lonely is thrown around a lot. Maybe it's time to see that a little differently. It doesn't have to be that way, and it's not a requirement of change that you will get lonely and outgrow everyone. If anything, it's you that will make it a lonely trip because you forget to invest in your relationships, and if anything, that only makes it more challenging because you will need support to make the changes you want.

You can put support into three simple categories. Emotional, informational and companionable. Emotional support comes from people who love you and offers affection, care, and compassion. Family, friends and partners are obvious providers of this. Informational support is from people who can help you with what you are trying to achieve, change or work on. Finally, companionship through shared social activities is crucial yet often neglected. You have home and work, but where do you feel you belong outside of home and work? Do you have a 'third place?' What's your thing? Where do you go for you? Do you have a hobby that you share with like-minded people?

Of course, these support networks don't come without a few common mistakes to navigate. For example, we often look to the people who support us emotionally, such as partners, to provide informational help. Of course, this is because we trust them. Yet, they are often the worst people to help us, either because they aren't qualified or because, as any coach knows, we won't take them seriously. In addition, they will generally love you so much that they end up talking you out of making changes; "Oh, you don't need to do that. I love you as you are". Separating those two will be crucial. And that often neglected third place, now that is something worth taking seriously.

So, when it comes to seeing greater so that you can be greater, don't forget the importance of other people in that vision you are creating. Remember that quality relationships are great for your health and well-being and offer vital support because the road to change isn't easy. Getting all these support systems in place and nurturing these relationships will be an important part of your vision; otherwise, the road to change will get lonely and challenging. Even worse, you may find that you haven't got many of the people you care about alongside you when you reach your destination.

It's still about you as well

All this talk about others makes it easy to think that you should put all your focus there, and here I am about to turn the tables on you with the subtle reminder that your relationships with others will be defined and shaped by the one that you have – yourself.

As with all things, it is balance that is crucial. Yes, make sure you build solid relationships and seek out quality connections with others. The benefits are undeniable, but you also work on yourself simultaneously. Working to deal with your personal shit gives you the potential for even greater relationships. Carl Jung once said (and I am seriously paraphrasing here) that what you refuse to face in yourself will be passed to others to deal with. This is a friendly reminder that the things you don't face up to often impact the people you hold dearest.

So, improving your relationships is good for you, and improving you is good for your relationships. Yes, the way you show up does impact others for better or worse, but (and I'm pretty passionate about this) don't work on yourself *for* others. Don't fall into the trap that so many of the motivational speakers out there promote when they say that you should be improving yourself and you should be 'doing it for your family'.

Do it for yourself

Using people you care about as your accountability is bullshit. The mantras I hear all the time in this industry drive me nuts: "find someone you are afraid of letting down" or "who are you letting down if you aren't at your best?" Using the people who you love and care about to shame yourself into some kind of action; how does that help you or them? It doesn't. Day after day I see people pedalling that message. As if you need something else to feel bad about!

I was chatting with my Mum about this book. She had serious mental health issues when I was younger, and she said:

> "I used to be petrified that I would make you the same way as me."

My mum wouldn't have needed someone to create more fear for her about impacting me. She was well aware of her impact on me, thank you very much. Extra accountability of this sort is nothing short of toxic. In extreme circumstances, people can see this as the reason not to be here "They would be better off without me". In a slightly less extreme example, this approach can lead to the "I am doing it for you" excuse that will come when you feel the need to justify your actions. Or feeling a lack of appreciation when the people you are 'doing it for' don't seem to quite get it. This can very quickly unravel your efforts to make changes to your life as your support networks and relationships start to break down.

All in all, shame-based motivation sucks. It's peddled to you by amateurs. When improving your relationship with yourself, do it for yourself and just remind yourself it benefits others. Do it for you but remember to build solid relationships while you are doing it.

What about the 'others'?

So, to recap, having other people in your life is essential. It is important that you avoid forgetting about your nearest and dearest in your pursuit of change, while ensuring you don't make the changes *for them*. Make changes *for yourself* as that way, everybody wins. That being said, not a week goes by when I don't get asked a question about dealing with other people. 'Other People' usually fall into four common categories: Negative people, people who mock you, criticise you, or offer unwanted advice and tell you what you should be doing.

Now, unlike all the popular advice out there (eye roll), I don't believe you have to get rid of these people from your life. After all, life would get pretty small and lonely if we went around removing everyone who was slightly annoying. 'Cancel culture' anyone? Counterproductive. If anything, having a few people about that irritate you is a brilliant chance to learn some stuff about yourself.

So how about those negative people that annoy us so much? What do you do with those people? First up, remember you *are* one of those people. Yes. Me, you and everyone else is negative at times. The funny thing is when you start to improve how you feel about yourself and your life, you begin to find people who aren't in the same place as you. Frustrating! Why? Well, in my experience, it's because you see what you don't like about yourself in them. You see in them the echoes of everything you have worked hard to change about yourself, and you don't like it. It's not negative people so much as negativity itself that you have the issue with. They are just a reminder of a quality you don't like.

The even weirder thing is, when you start and aren't doing so great, you tend to find that people who are happy and positive can annoy you as well. That's the flip side of the same coin, because you are seeing them as a reminder of what you don't have. Want to know the common denominator? You. So generally, other people can't win. They can't win because it is you who has the issues here. Which is brilliant because you can change that.

That is unless you do what the self-help industry advises you to and cut out all the so-called negative people from your life. This by the way, allows you to get away with not owning the fact that you too can be negative. This tactic is probably one of the primary reasons many people who start improving themselves and their life end up alone on that journey. As Socrates said, "How can you wonder if your travels do you no good, when you carry yourself around with you? You are saddled with the very thing that drove you away."

Negativity isn't a bad thing, either. After all, would you cut out the negative person going through a rough time just now, who simply hasn't had that 'right!' moment where they know they need to do something about it? Would you suggest I cut out all the negative people who come into my world, as they must be a drain on my energy?

Are these people taking your energy and happiness away, or are you giving it away?

Read that again. I'd say you are giving it away. You are giving it away by fighting against what you see in front of you. When something outside of me has such an effect on my nervous system that it changes how I feel, it's something to enquire about within myself. So, what do you do about negative people? Accept you are one as well; concentrate on how you are showing up and go from there.

Of course, it's not always negative people that can get to us. You will also get lots of unwanted advice in your life. Don't confuse this with criticism. We will come to that later. Unwanted advice is everywhere, with people telling you what you should or shouldn't do. It can get annoying, yet it usually comes from one of two places. Either the person giving it has some genuine advice that will help us. Or it's them telling us what **they** need to hear. Unwanted advice is often the advice the person giving it needs to hear. It comes back to that wonderful principle that what you see in other people, even what they should or shouldn't do, is inside us too. So, what can you do with unwanted advice? Well, first up ask if it's helpful. If it is, then excellent; apply it if you want. The second thing is to ask:

"is this advice for me or actually for them?"

If it's for them, it's a case of smiling back and remembering we are all doing our best.

Some folks, on the other hand, will just be critical. You know how it is, constantly putting you down, always finding fault, and that is a tough place to be on the receiving end of. We are pretty good at putting ourselves down, so having someone else do it is not helping matters. Like all things, the key is to remember that we all criticise: we criticise others, and we criticise ourselves. Sometimes people aren't criticising you. You just take it that way, which is often a sign that you're a tad insecure about what they are talking about. Other times they may well be criticising you. Why? Because they are generally unhappy.

When anyone is unhappy, they look to make themselves feel better in some way, and at times that way is by criticising other people. When facing criticism, it's handy to remind yourself to ask if they have a point. This is a tricky one, but it's a time when it pays to be really honest with yourself. If it hurts you, is it because they have a point? Is it something you need to work on? If you can honestly say that as far as you can see it is not true, then remind yourself that the criticism isn't about you, it's about them.

As the saying goes, 'hurt people, hurt people'. Very often, their criticism of you is their unhappiness projected onto you. It doesn't make it OK, yet it will stop you from making it personal, and that is how criticism can start to bounce off you

This brings us to mocking; mocking is that sneaky facet of all of this. It generally happens when you are starting to change things. You may begin to give up some old habits that have been holding you back, you may begin to do new things, and the people around you start taking the mick a little and they start to mock. Why? Well, by now, it's probably pretty obvious. We mock something when we feel put out by it. Maybe it's a bit of envy or a lack of understanding. Very often though, it's when you start to make changes in your life that the people around you can begin to feel a little insecure about where they are themselves. To deal with that, they mock the thing they believe is causing it: you and your new behaviours.

Mocking, in my experience, always comes from insecurity. The question I always pose when people ask me how to deal with family and friends mocking them is, why does it bother you so much? Possibly because you are insecure about what they are mocking you about. As always, when it comes to people, it's generally about them, but it is important that you can also see that it's about you as well. If you are secure in what you are doing, then mocking may be mildly annoying, but it won't derail your efforts to change.

When it comes to the other people in your life, it's worth remembering that you cannot control what they say or how they are. All you can control is how you respond. If you want to get better at that, then a great place to start is to see the difficult people you come into contact with as an opportunity to learn about yourself. In doing so, you may even keep some of the relationships that would otherwise have fallen apart.

The lighthouse versus the tugboat

You might be wondering 'what about the people I care about?'

It's natural to want to help and inspire the people you love and care about to live a full and happy life. You may see them struggling and want to help them, think they are capable of more and push them or you start to feel better and want everyone to feel that way.

"My partner needs this…"

"My kids really need this…"

…become the things you start saying, and overnight you morph into a cheap version of the Dalai Lama. You start to tell them how they should think and what they need to do. It comes from love, and you honestly believe they hear:

"I love you and want to help you feel better…"

Very often, though, they hear:

"I want you to be different…"

or

"I want you to change…"

Being a coach has drawbacks, and it's very easy to go into coach mode with friends and family. I spend my life coaching people so it comes naturally to want to help others, yet to help others you really need their permission. I remember one day someone saying to me:

"I need a friend... not a coach, Si."

So, how can you go about helping without coming across as if you think you know best or that your loved ones 'need help'? The possible answer lies in a well-talked-about analogy: The lighthouse versus the tugboat. It's based upon the saying 'be the change you wish to see in the world' and the two ways you can achieve that. The ships crash into the rocks and the tugboat goes out there, saves the day and pulls them into shore. It's hard work using all that energy to save the ships and getting battered out there in the storms. We can often be tugboats, telling everyone how to live, trying to force them into feeling better and steering their lives for them.

You become a tugboat when you try to convince the people closest to you how they should live and when you tell them what they need to do. Tugboats are out there trying to save everyone and convince people through sheer determination that their way is the only way. Social media is full of tugboats. You can see it in the arguments in the comments sections, each attacking the other's viewpoint whilst stating how theirs is the superior one. In most cases, this advice comes from a good place since you want people to see a better way, yet all it does is cause people to stick to their guns. The more someone's beliefs get attacked, the harder they defend them. To get technical, that's a brain bias called the 'backfire effect'. When someone gets challenged over what they believe, this challenge often only serves to actually to strengthen their beliefs, not weaken them.

So, what do lighthouses do? They help ships navigate the rocky coastline, yet they do it by standing still, shining their light and illuminating the obstacles, dangers and the clearer path. The ships can see and follow that or do what they want.

Either way, the lighthouse is there doing its own thing whether it has a receptive audience or not. That is the way to go about helping the people around us: the negative people, the struggling people, the people you love and care about, the person at work who's down in the dumps and your kids.

Be a lighthouse.

Live your life fully. Embody what you believe in. That is you shining that light. When it shines long enough, people either follow and see the fruits of your labour as something they want, or they too start to find their path. Lighthouses are who they want to be whilst allowing others the same choices. Yes, maybe those people you care about will make mistakes, and perhaps they will hit setbacks, but the more you try and remove those obstacles for them the more their own personal spark dies out. They also need to forge their own path, learning as they go. That passivity takes discipline and understanding on your part. It's easy to tugboat the people you love and want to help, yet all that happens is you burn out, and they either resist or forever become dependent on you. Be a lighthouse, follow your path and let your light help others find theirs.

Try not to care too much

Being a lighthouse isn't easy. We would all be out there being the change if it was. In truth, everything in the following chapters will help you do this in some way. Something to be hugely aware of, though, is *'overcare'*. You are taught that the more you care the better things go, or the more you care the better a person you are. Yet care isn't that simple. Like all things, there is a balance to be had.

Let's think about care for a minute. Care should do two things: nourish the object of our care and, at the same time, nourish us. Overcare is when you care too much about something or someone and no longer nourish them or yourself, which is unhealthy. When you over care about something, your sense of worth tends to get tied up in that thing. You can't separate your identity from that external, perceived measure of your personal success. You start to create this situation where your identity is tied up directly with how that thing is going. So, if it's all going well then you are OK. When it isn't, you aren't, so your sense of worth starts to rise and fall with how the thing you care about is going. That tends to lead people to try to control everything, as they need it all to look and behave a certain way in order to be happy.

Finally, when you over care about something so much that you apply huge amounts of significance to it, you create anxiety around it. So, all in all, overcare can lead to a lot of unnecessary stress, control issues, anxiety, panic and, yes, our old friend burnout.

The person who overcares about their kids is constantly stressed and anxious and suffocates them. We all know that parent who lives through their children's achievements. This not only denies that parent's individual spark, as their identity is inexorably tied to their children but often, sadly quenches the spark of those kids through overcontrol and unreasonable expectation.

The person who overcares about getting that job gets so ramped up that they cock up the interview and get nowhere. The person who overcares about their health becomes obsessive and starts to create ill health in the process. The person who overcares about what other people think about them creates enormous amounts of insecurity and worry in themselves and tends to need a huge amount of reassurance from others.

Overcare is a nightmare, yet we are taught to wear it like a badge of honour. It's important to understand that by not over caring, I don't mean not caring at all. So, what is the answer? Again, our unreliable method is to go from one extreme to another. That is the cycle we tend to move through, as we go from over-caring about something or someone to completely burning out and not caring at all. That cycle alone is exhausting.

The answer is finding the appropriate level of care, which is what lighthouses do well. Care should nourish the person or object of your care, not create huge spikes of stress and anxiety in us and suffocate them.

Here is the thing: when it comes to other people, lighthouses care for their kids at a level that encourages them but doesn't stop them from living their own life. They love the other people in their life enough to allow them their freedom. They care about what others think and therefore listen and take on board opinions without taking it personally.

When it comes to their ambitions in life, lighthouses care about their health enough to improve it, but not to let it affect other areas of life. They care enough about their career to take pride in their performance but not let it take over, and they care enough about themselves without taking themselves too seriously.

They also get a lot wrong but learn from those mistakes because they care enough to develop and grow from them. When you find yourself over caring, what do you do? How do you behave? What behaviours are the ones that become un-healthy? From there, what could you do instead? What would a healthier level of care look like in that area?

Caring just enough is tricky. I wish I could say I get it right all the time. I don't. Being a lighthouse is hard. Being the change, you want to see without forcing it on others takes skill. To dance to your tune without needing everyone else to join in. Yet it may well be the greatest way of living. None of us is perfect, and none of us ever will be. Yet with time and patience, you can come to understand yourself and who you are. You can set out to be that person, build a life, make connections with others, and navigate the world you live in and the problems it sends your way with some skill, grace and humility.

Try this

Grab a pen and paper and your mobile phone. The following steps are all straightforward ways that you can start to bring others back into your life, improve your energy levels and relationships and upgrade your support networks. As always, it will take a bit of effort on your part. Nothing changes without some practical action, and these three simple, easy-to-do things will make a massive difference in your life.

Step 1: Reach out and engage

    A. Think of someone who has really helped you at some point in your life.

    B. Reach out and thank them via message now. Tell them what they did, how it helped you, and how grateful you are.

C. Think of a friend in your life.

D. Message them and remind them of a nice memory you have had together. Tell them you were thinking about it, and it made you smile.

E. Write a note for a loved one – a child, partner or anyone like that. Tell them you love them.

F. Leave it somewhere where they will find it in the morning.

Step 2: Improve your support levels

A. Look at the following support areas. Ask yourself how supported you feel in each area and give a score out of five. One means not at all, five means 100% supported.

Emotional: empathy, concern, affection, love, trust, acceptance, intimacy, encouragement, or caring

My score: _____

Informational: advice, guidance, suggestions, or useful information in areas you want to improve

My score: _____

Companionship: social belonging via shared hobbies and activities

My score: _____

B. What areas score the lowest and need to improve?

C. Write down some ideas of what you could do to improve that area

Step 3: How can you care more appropriately?

A. Look across your life at relationships, hobbies, and goals. What areas or people are you caught up in over caring about?

B. How does that overcare affect you, it or them in a negative way?

C. How could you start displaying a more appropriate care level? What could you do less of or more of?

At this point, you may have more of an idea of what you want.

You know the importance of other people in life, as well as how to deal with the negativity of some.

You will also have some awareness of your need to change some people around you. From here, it is time to put the focus back on you.

It is time to focus on building your own energy mentally, emotionally and physically. Even more importantly, it's time to see how burnout will keep you stuck.

A quick recap

Don't underestimate the importance of your connections with other people in your quest for change. The quality of those connections is important. Lack of care, overcare or having poor and toxic relationships will impact your well-being.

1. Don't forget to include other people in your vision for life. Quality relationships are the number one factor in the quality of your life as you age. You are wired for connection with other people.

2. When it comes to relationships, quality beats quantity. High-conflict relationships are toxic to your well-being. Relationships with people we know we can count on are where the magic is.

3. Loneliness is toxic. Support is crucial to your success in changing things in life. The three critical types of support are emotional, informational and companionship.

4. You can care too much. Consider how that shows up for you and adjust to a healthier, more appropriate behaviour so that both you and the object of your care can benefit.

5. When dealing with others, remember it's very often the case that we can solve it by seeking to understand both ourselves and their position in life.

6. When it comes to helping others you care about, try to adopt the lighthouse approach; it will save you energy and increase the chance they will find their own way.

PART 2

Feel Greater...

4

NOTHING IS MORE IMPORTANT THAN HOW YOU FEEL

Back in 2012, things were a bit of a mess for me. I don't think many people realised as I have always been half decent at putting on a good front. Things on the outside would have looked OK, but it was a different story on the inside. Anxiety was crippling me, negative thoughts, self-loathing, and insecurity were all floating about, and I just wanted more out of my life. I remember being asked:

> "if you had a magic wand, what one thing would you fix?"

The answer was simple. I would turn my brain off. Stop it chattering away at me. The trouble was, no matter how disruptive it got, I could never seem to get motivated to do the things I was told would help. I'd lost that drive.

You may be able to relate to no longer finding much, if any, enjoyment in the things you used to love doing and becoming more cynical about life. Hating being around people, and yet not liking being with yourself either. You are undoubtedly trying. You read the right books, watch YouTube videos, follow inspiring people on social media, download all the breathing apps, and set goals. Yet if you are like most people, you keep hitting the same roadblock. You feel OK for a little, manage to get going and then run out of steam.

At times it felt like I was feeling worse rather than better, despite everything I was doing.

Then one day I picked up an article about burnout in the workplace. It said ***burnout is a state of physical and emotional exhaustion***. It can occur when you experience long-term stress in your job or have worked in a physically or emotionally draining role for a long time. Now, I wasn't in a stressful job, yet when I read the listed symptoms – feeling tired or drained most of the time, feeling helpless, trapped and defeated, feeling detached/alone in the world, having a cynical/negative outlook, self-doubt, procrastinating and taking longer to get things done, feeling overwhelmed –well, I had all of them. Here is the even more interesting bit.

In a study conducted in 2019, 68% of people mistakenly labelled their burnout as anxiety.

(Mental Health UK)

I knew I was burnt out, and I knew I was physically, mentally and emotionally stressed out. You may believe that your negative thoughts are always the cause of your stress and anxiety, I was the same – and you can't be faulted for accepting this widespread view. We all see calls to 'Stop negative thinking!'

and 'Control your thoughts and feel free!' all over the place. Well, this is a bit of a simplistic way to look at things. Popular opinion has led most of you to view yourselves as a bit of a brain on a stick; that all communication flows down from your brain to everything else, and therefore if you think bad, you feel bad.

However, this is a misconception. Rather than thinking of ourselves as a one-way street with everything starting in the brain and working its way down, it is better to picture a two-way flow of information. Consider the systems in your body at work: your heart, your breathing and your digestive system (to name but a few), all feeding information up to the brain, which is weighing that information up. If all that information 'going up' is informing the brain that the gut, the heart, the lungs or whatever are chronically stressed and not performing well, then your brain, in simple terms, starts freaking out a little. The brain has now been told that things aren't all as they should be and starts looking for reasons why. Simply trying to sort the brain (your thinking) out isn't going to do much if the rest of you is not functioning well.

So, when it comes to being greater than your current reality — *You can't be greater if you can't feel greater.* How you feel affects how you think, the decisions you make, the actions you take and the behaviours you form. You can try and wrestle with those and spend vast amounts of energy fighting the symptoms, or you can get to the root cause, overcome burnout, and start feeling better first. To do that, you will want to begin recognising burnout and learning not only how to recover from it but stop yourself from going there in the first place.

It may be 'normal' but it's not healthy

'You talk about burnout as if it's something new; it's natural to feel that way in life.' Someone sent me that message on social media after I had run one of our courses. In one sense, I agree. Burnout is not a new concept. However, it's the word 'natural' with which I can't agree. I think what people often mean by 'natural' is 'normal' and what they mean by 'normal' is 'common'. Yes, it's common to feel burnt out now. It's common to feel chronically anxious, overwhelmed, unmotivated and stressed. All these things are common today, but they are not natural and nor should they be normalised! This book is about ending this cycle while at the same time saying it's not your fault. You lack the skills needed to navigate your life. Don't feel that you simply need to manage that. You can be free of it, and you can be free of long-term, ongoing, (chronic) emotional and mental chaos.

The interesting thing about burnout is that it's been shown that people do normalise it. You just think, 'This is just how it is'. You can't remember not feeling this way. So, you start to justify it. Maybe society encourages us to wear exhaustion with a sort of skewed pride. We all love to tell people how tired and hardworking we are. I'm sure society believes, on some level, that the harder you work and the more you burn yourself out the more deserving you are of a better life. Humans are such resourceful creatures that you can normalise anything to cope, even things like obesity and ill health or abuse in relationships. We are great normalisers, and that isn't always helpful.

The trouble is burnout causes enormous problems for you. If you are burnt out, your amygdala (the brain's fear centre) enlarges, becoming more hyper-vigilant, looking for more problems and being on high alert. It is scanning non-stop for threats and potential danger. Even worse, burnout fractures the connectivity between the amygdala and the thinking centres of the brain. So not only are you experiencing more fear, but you are also less able to reason it out, meaning you become much more irrational.

Irrational thinking makes it harder to unlearn fear-based memories resulting in trauma, and any stressful experiences from your past are harder to let go of. Mind wandering increases, meaning your attention is pulled all over the shop by anything and everything, spiking anxiety, panic and mental exhaustion. It's easy to see when you read that back just how many of the issues you suffer with today are, in some way, related to burnout. In addition, burnout isn't helping you to move past your issues, no matter how hard you work.

One of the first steps to removing burnout from your life is to stop accepting it as normal and so no longer justify it as a natural part of life. This takes a paradigm shift in how you think. Feeling chronically exhausted is not 'just life', and it certainly isn't 'just the way it is'. Nor is it something you should expect, tolerate and get on with. It is none of these things, but rather it is something you can monitor in yourself and mitigate.

Is stress normal? Of course. Stress is not bad, as you will learn later in this book. Chronic, prolonged stress is what we are trying to avoid. The type of stress that breaks you down over time and makes you weaker, not stronger. So, don't for a minute think I am saying avoid all stress in your life. The message is to prevent long-term chronic stress, avoid unnecessary stress and avoid plunging yourself into a state of complete and utter mental and physical exhaustion, just because that is considered normal. You deserve better than that.

How did we get here?

Burnout is a state of physical, mental and emotional exhaustion and it is caused by long-term, chronic stress. Of course, the chronic exhaustion that comes with burnout results from the 'running on empty' examples I discussed earlier. You struggle to prioritise your well-being, put yourself last on the list each day and generally burn yourself into the ground. All this just by trying to keep up with life and often your unreasonable demands upon yourself.

However, running on empty is not the only trigger for burnout. Most of the work on the subject has been studied in workplaces, with Professor Christina Maslach being the real authority. In studies led by her, it was found that there were some common triggers for burnout:

Lack of control – A feeling you don't have control over your tasks and outcomes

Lack of reward – Be it pay, appreciation, chances of promotion and so on.

Lack of community – Lack of quality social interactions and support.

Lack of fairness – A sense of being treated unfairly.

Values clashes - When our values clash with those of the workplace.

Work overload - Doing too much.

Although most of the work on burnout has been conducted in the workplace, we see many of these triggers in daily life through our work at Unbreakable.

How often do you feel you lack control over the outcomes of things in your relationships? How often do you feel under-rewarded through a lack of appreciation from the people you care about? We have already discussed how toxic feeling lonely can be and how lacking social connection is not great for your health and well-being. Many of us feel unfairly treated, very often by life itself. Values clashes are everywhere in families and are incredibly common on social media. At the time of writing, we have not been out of lockdown for very long. The Covid pandemic went on for two years; how many triggers can you recognise for yourself coming out of that alone? I'm sure you were very much in situations out of your control. Businesses collapsed through no fault of the people involved, and your social support may have dwindled as people stayed at home. Values clashes were everywhere, and now, as we are coming out the other end, people are reporting burnout and struggling to get back into the swing of life.

So yes, burnout is often work-related, yet work isn't the only catalyst for chronic stress. So much of life can, by its nature, drain you of your energy and cause chronic stress. Parenting, caring for elderly relatives, maintaining meaningful relationships, trauma from loss, abuse, ill-health, and so on. Of course, you can't avoid these triggers; they are a part of life. The key is noticing them and having the skills to deal with them because when you are aware of what could be causing your chronic stress, you can start to limit it at the source. When you deal with that, you have the power to limit the effects it has upstream. In this case, the way you are feeling, thinking and behaving.

It's amazing how many messages I get when discussing this subject. The sheer relief people feel when they see that they aren't broken and that there is an answer. When it comes to improving how you feel, being aware of the common triggers that, over time, can push you into burnout can be a lifesaver because now you can stop them at the source, so to speak. You can stop fighting against the feelings of burnout, and you can get to the root cause of it in your life. You can start to deal with the triggers (we give you a handy skill to try out in the 'try this' section for that), or if they can't be dealt with, learn to manage them efficiently. Two ways to go with burnout are navigating it with understanding and skill or fighting against it. Unfortunately, fighting against the results of burnout is why you will experience a lot of stop-starting on the path to creating a better life for yourself.

Fighting, controlling and making it all worse

Before we discuss how to end the burnout cycle, we will look at common mistakes people make that contribute to worsening burnout's effects.

When I was a younger lad and in possession of hair and moderate good looks, I wanted to get in shape. I was a small kid, and I was skinny. Now, as a young man that never felt too good, and as I was into football and training and loved running and sport, I thought I would get into lifting weights. Off I went to research how to get bigger. Of course, that search led to bodybuilding. We didn't have a computer at home back then. It was back when the internet was a rare thing to have at home, and if you did, it was dial-up and you couldn't use the phone at the same time. Crazy times. So, it was all about magazines. Off I went and bought Flex Magazine, and there were those routines: 'Jay Cutler's Mass Plan', 'Get Shredded' and stuff like that. In my young and naive thinking, Jay looked big and I wanted to be big, so I should follow his plan.

So off I trot into my garage gym of a little bench and some of my older brother's weights. The next day I felt like I could barely move, and the thought of walking, let alone training again that week, was beyond my imagination. I soon realised that what helps a steroid-enhanced professional bodybuilder win Mr Olympia wasn't what a 17-year-old, 9-stone dripping wet boy needed. It was too much.

Getting out of burnout is the same. You have to be very careful how you go about it. One way you might get it wrong is to add more chronic stress to your already chronically stressed system. I made that mistake early. Waking up each day and literally trying to outrun my feelings by running. When those incredible endorphins wore off I felt even more exhausted than when I began.

You may have noticed by now, many of the 'gurus' and 'influencers' at the top of this Personal Development Industry, that I am a part of, really grind my gears.

This type of attack approach is peddled by so many of them. They are taking chronically stressed and burnt-out people and encouraging them to set massive goals, take huge, inspired action, to out-act their overwhelm and fears on a daily basis. It's the equivalent of my 17-year-old self taking Jay Cutler's plan and wondering why I couldn't train like a pro bodybuilder. Adding extra chronic stress on top of a chronically stressed person is, at best, not practical and at worst disastrous. Sure, it sounds good, and sure the person who gives this advice to you does it with confidence. Yet it's not effective in the long run. Most people believe that when their motivation stalls (cue more feelings of guilt and shame) usually, it is simply exhaustion (cue more anxiety; spiked by that exhaustion).

Psychologist Mihaly Csikszentmihalyi was arguably the godfather of 'flow', a state of joy, creativity and total involvement, in which problems seem to disappear, and there is an exhilarating feeling of transcendence. Think 'in the zone,' that fantastic feeling when you are wholly absorbed in something, you don't think of anything else, and time seems to disappear. In this state, your performance rockets because your focus increases and your brain chemistry really works for you. Athletes, artists and performers often report experiencing this state, and you will have experienced it countless times while engaging in the simplest of things.

His research has been phenomenal. One theory he pioneered was called 'The Challenge to Skills Ratio'. This theory is based on the fact that if the challenge of a task far outweighs your skills, it will trigger anxiety and overwhelm you. Equally, if the challenge is way below your skills, you will quickly get bored and lose enthusiasm. Csikszentmihalyi believed that the optimal level for performance and focus is a challenge that slightly outweighs your skills; that is the sweet spot for performance.

If you are trying to get stronger and go to the gym, you don't pick a weight you can handle with your eyes closed because it doesn't challenge you enough. You will find it too easy and lose focus. At the same time, you don't want to pick a weight you can't lift, because now you either get injured or simply can't perform the exercise at all. You are much better off choosing a challenging weight that makes you work, but that you can manage.

You will want to consider your approach to your mind and your life that way. Are you picking the weight you can lift, is your plan causing you more overwhelm and anxiety than is necessary? Is it giving you a fighting chance to win, or is it setting you up for failure from the off? The belief that the bigger the goal, the more motivating it will be or the more progress you will make is a falsehood. The key to transforming any area of your life will be what you do consistently, and being consistent will come down to how you manage that ratio in your life.

Does this mean you shouldn't set lofty visions for yourself? After all, the first section of this book was about creating a vision for your life that inspires and motivates you. The simple answer is yes, set visions as big as you like, but learn how to manage them. Chunk them down to weekly or daily steps that you are confident you can perform, ones that stretch you but don't snap you. As always, the skill is in the dosage.

Most of us have been there. On Monday, you decide that you will live like a monk as well as a professional athlete and overhaul your life in one day, only to run out of steam by Wednesday. On Wednesday night, you have quit, and you are eating and drinking your feelings of 'failure'. By Friday, as well as feeling more shit, you also start feeling unmotivated and bored as you have no challenge going on at all anymore. You have bounced from setting yourself a challenge that is too hard and induces burnout to one that is way below your skill level and is now wholly unmotivating. So, when it comes to burnout, anxiety and overwhelm, it's not your fault that you have been stuck in that cycle. Many of the methods you are being shown simply aren't going to help you move past it. If anything, they are going to push you further into it. So, give yourself a break, dust yourself off and get ready to learn a new way of feeling better.

Eat first or starve

The King or Queen eats first is a popular personal development saying. Some of you may have heard it, and some of you who are new to this may not. I'll be honest, I'm not much into the whole King and Queen thing. However, it serves a purpose here. By now, you may be starting to see that the root cause of most anxiety, motivation and feeling stuck scenarios will be burnout brought on by prolonged chronic stress. That stress has completely frazzled your nervous system, which is now running on high alert. It's making you feel exhausted, unmotivated and helpless.

There are many routes to burnout. All those triggers that cause you chronic stress show up, and yet before you start looking at that, one way you put yourself into chronic stress is to not look after yourself.

We often tend to put ourselves last on our list of priorities. I get it. We all do it, and at times it's necessary to help someone you love to push through a project or help someone out. But if you do this continuously, without taking some time to look after yourself, you will reach a breaking point where you have nothing left. It's one of the reasons that many caregivers to people they love end up ill themselves. It's why people in professions dealing with other people's pain can start experiencing compassion fatigue, where they lose empathy for other people's problems.

I'm sure many coaches wouldn't admit that, but in my own life, I'll be honest, this has undoubtedly been an issue I have had to deal with.

If burnout comes from prolonged stress, not looking after yourself over time certainly leads to that. Unfortunately, a great level of well-being doesn't just happen, it needs to be created to some extent. You have to make it happen proactively. It's where the idea that the King/Queen eats first comes in. You have to eat. You have to serve yourself so you can help others. After all, you can't give what you don't have. You like to think you can, but you can't. So, what stops you from 'eating first'? One primary reason that stops many is that you think you have unlimited energy each day, so you can keep drawing down on that, and it will always be there. Then one day, it just isn't, and then you start to normalise that feeling and fall into that trap of accepting chronic exhaustion as the status quo.

One of the most significant shifts you can make to your thinking is to see energy less like something you have infinite amounts of, and more like something you have only so much of, like money.

Most of you treat cash with much more respect than your energy, because you know that you only have so much. You are also aware of the issues around not having enough. So, you spend it wisely and you try to add more to your account to have more to spend, or to have should you need it on a rainy day. In many ways, you treat money with more importance than your energy because you feel energy is something you always have unlimited amounts of – but you don't.

For a moment, just imagine that you have three energy bank accounts, a physical, a mental, and an emotional one. You spend from these accounts all day, yet each one only has so much in it. The more you spend and the less you top them up, the more they decline. Sure, they may top up a bit overnight with a decent night's sleep, but if that is all you do to add to them, eventually you start each day with less than you had before. All of a sudden, you are overdrawn and being overdrawn creates a state of chronic daily stress for you. When the 'rainy day' hits, you simply don't have the energy resources backed up to deal with it. Add to that, making changes in your life will take energy, and if you only have enough to cope with the current demands of your day-to-day life, how will you have enough to go and make the changes required? You won't, and this is where many come unstuck; you simply don't have enough in the tanks to deal with life and make the changes you want. Topping up those back accounts is crucial, and that's what I mean by 'eating first'. Top up your accounts, because if you don't you won't have anything left to draw on when you need it, and you certainly won't have enough to go out and make changes.

Of course, you could top up your energy accounts all day and still end up overdrawn, and that is where looking at energy as money comes in again. Much like money, you want to be aware that you only have so much to spend, so spending it on important things is crucial. If you only had £50 to feed your family this month, you probably wouldn't spend it all in one night on a takeaway. You would budget and spread it out. The question now becomes, how can you start to eat first? Can you take 15 minutes a day to top up your energy accounts? Why not start there? At this point you may begin to find reasons you can't. I get it; we all do it. You may think, "Surely that's selfish? People need me.", and there is an element of truth to that. But it is time to stop using them as the reason you can't look after yourself and more as a reminder of why it is important to. No one is asking you to up sticks and move across the world for a

6-month retreat. Start simple. 15 minutes a day. I know you can find that.

Try this

Grab a pen and paper. It is time to start moving you away from burnout. The steps below are all awareness exercises that will take no time. By the end, you will be aware of your burnout triggers, how you top up and spend your energy, and how at risk of burnout you are, which are all vital steps in starting to feel better.

Step 1: Become aware of your triggers

A. Rate the following triggers out of 5.
    1 = not at all, 5 = extremely often.

    Lack of control: a feeling that you don't have control over your tasks and outcomes.

    Lack of reward: be it pay, appreciation, chances of promotion and so on.

    Lack of community: insufficient quality social interactions and support.

    Lack of fairness: a sense of being treated unfairly.

    Values clashes: when your values clash with those of the workplace.

    Work overload: doing too much.

B. Look at your highest trigger score. What could you do to deal with that trigger?

Step 2: Improve your investments

A. Divide a piece of paper in half with low quality on the left side and high quality on the right.

B. Write down all the low-quality investments you make energy-wise, down the left side. Be extremely honest and think of all the things you do mentally, emotionally and physically that don't help you.

C. Look at each low-quality answer you wrote down. Think of a more useful one that's higher quality.

D. Pick one and go do it now. Literally now.

E. Pick one to do tomorrow and set a reminder on your phone.

STEP 3: See how at risk of burnout you really are

Becoming aware of burnout and how it can affect your life is a big eye-opener for most people. Simply knowing what it is can be a relief, finally having an answer to why you feel the way you do. Awareness is the first step; it's time to get into how you can start to get out of burnout, protect yourself from it and control how you feel. Visit: www.bit.ly/htbls-quiz or scan the QR Code below with your phone's camera, and it will open a quiz that will tell you how at risk of or how deep into burnout you are:

A quick recap

Burnout is not 'normal' or 'just a part of life'. Continually replenishing your energy accounts is vital when it comes to mitigating the effects of burnout.

1. Change requires you to feel greater than you do now. Nothing changes until we start to feel better first because how we feel dictates how we think and behave.

2. A tremendous amount of stress, anxiety, overwhelm and lack of motivation is caused by being burnt out; they are often the symptoms, and burnout is the root cause.

3. You must stop normalising exhaustion and chronic stress. It may be common, but it's not helpful or natural. It's breaking you down. It is not making you stronger.

4. Common triggers to burnout: lack of control or reward, unfair treatment, values clashes, lack of community and support, and work overload create long-term stress in an unhealthy way if not managed.

5. You can worsen burnout by taking on challenges too big and trying to outfight them. Create plans and challenges that stretch you rather than snap you, and you will get stronger and achieve more success.

6. Think of energy like money, not as something infinite in your life. Top up regularly and spend it wisely because the better you manage and invest, the better you will feel, perform and handle change.

5

RECOVER LIKE YOUR LIFE DEPENDS ON IT

"Rest is not a reward, it's a requirement."

...is a saying that, to my mind, is 100% true. We often look at rest as a reward reserved for after working hard and completing the job. We feel like rest needs to be deserved or earned in some way. Biologically speaking, quality rest is essential for us to perform at our best. So, if you are burnt out and running on empty, then rest and recovery will of course be helpful.

But what kind of rest and recovery?

When you are tired you may think doing nothing will be the answer. That is what you may call passive recovery. Passive recovery could be looked at like sedation. It's when you watch TV mindlessly, binge-watch an entire series in one day, play on your phone for hours and eat rubbish while lazing on the sofa. It's not necessarily a bad thing in small doses, but the trouble with passive recovery is that it does very little for you.

It doesn't add to your energy levels, and it doesn't shift how you feel and think. Passive recovery is simply turning your brain off mindlessly. The thing with doing that is the more exhausted you become, the longer you take to recover, and the more you recover passively, the less energy you have. It's a cycle that feeds itself. In passive recovery mode, your energy levels do not regenerate sufficiently. Contrary to what you may think, lounging about, drinking, eating and snoozing the weekends away in front of the telly can increase burnout as time passes.

So, what's the alternative? Active recovery. Active recovery includes things that shift the way you feel, your mood and thoughts to a better place. Active recovery adds to your energy accounts. I'm sure you have been tired and had to force yourself to go for a walk or exercise, and afterwards you felt much more energetic and in higher spirits.

In that sense humans are like a car battery. You charge up by being used. Active recovery involves things like exercise, walking, training, stretching, yoga, massage, extreme heat like saunas and steam rooms, or extreme cold like cold showers and ice baths. It can also be things like socialising, hobbies, music, play just for the sake of play or a great film you are looking forward to. Even a decent night's sleep or a little nap are all forms of active recovery. After all, sleep is an incredibly involved process as all sorts of things are going on in your body while you slumber!

Active recovery is crucial to build into your life as it adds to your energy, helps your nervous system recover, fills up your tanks, and you then truly recover. Liken the difference between passive and active recovery to going to the gym to get stronger. When you lift weights you tear muscle fibres, and those fibres should repair and get stronger when you recover. If your recovery approach is passive you don't see much adaptation.

Your energy is much the same. You constantly put stressors on it when you recover passively. You don't come back stronger you come back weaker. Active recovery leaves you stronger and with more in the tank. Most people I see in coaching are getting energetically weaker as the months go by, until they end up with nothing left, and this is often purely down to using too much passive recovery.

I don't think you need to live like a monk, though! Some brilliant things to plug into your life and help you recover are walks in nature, time with family, playing with your kids, and meeting up with friends. Going phone free for a day and visiting somewhere new or going out for a nice meal, cooking, gardening, listening to music, playing an instrument or any skill or hobby. People also include meditation, float tanks, yoga and stretching etc. There is so much that you can do to introduce active recovery into your life.

So, before we get into all the daily habits of looking after your energy, it's worth looking at your time off and how you are spending it. Can you create weekends that give you more energy back than you put out? Can you get out in nature, walk, arrange something social, cook your favourite meal, meet a friend, go somewhere new or try something different? How can you start to make your time off enjoyable? Something that leaves you feeling better, not worse, come Monday morning?

Topping up the tank

You can barely move without someone telling you about the importance of a morning routine these days. Let's be honest, as dull and repetitive as that message is, it's a great start to any day. Topping up your energy accounts daily is vital if you want to feel better, especially if you need to get yourself out of burn-out. You can fill your weekends with the amazing active recovery we spoke about earlier. But, if you leave it only until then, you end up simply living for the weekend and trying desperately to claw back some energy every six days, before you start again on Monday.

Daily deposits into those physical, mental and emotional bank accounts are crucial. Does that mean you must spend hours a day preparing yourself? Not at all. You don't have to drag yourself out of bed three hours before work and put yourself through hours of rituals to get the best out of the day. If anything, that will increase your anxiety and stress, mainly because you are stressed about getting it all done. Quality over quantity is key. Plus, there is the rest of the day. You can always get some good stuff squeezed into your day before bed, which may be the most important time of day.

At the end of this chapter, you will get some straightforward and powerful morning and pre-sleep routines to help you top up your energy accounts and some things you can try throughout your day. Like everything, we tend to know what to do and just don't do it. I think that is because we don't understand how vital these things are or if they make that much difference. Well, they do! Read on.

Physically. you can top up your accounts with decent movement each day. I don't mean like a pro athlete; I mean decent movement for you. Of course, you know this, but how often are you doing it? Getting 20 minutes (in one go or broken up) of decent intensity exercise each day has shown to help a great deal in our courses. Often people think they need to do hours of exercise or go to the gym, but you don't, and there are loads of ways to get your heart rate up for 20 minutes each day.

Hydration

Hydration is another vitally important staple. It is the easiest to plug into your day. Again, people underestimate water's huge impact on us and don't bother. It's easy to say "yeah, yeah, I know", but most people I meet in our work are under-moving and dehydrated. Hydration makes a massive difference. Dehydration can cause brain fog and a feeling of tiredness in itself.

Nutrition

The same is the case with food. We often forget how dramatically food can alter our mood. I know that if I don't eat enough, I can get a feeling of stress and anger, and many people really are fuelling their bodies poorly. You can alter the quality of your thoughts and feelings, without eating and training like an Olympic Athlete. Simply eating two to three decent meals, drinking at least two litres of water and getting 20 minutes of movement each day can dramatically shift your mood and energy. Even better, you are already eating and drinking, so it's a case of continuing to do that but in a bit of a less shit way.

Appreciation and gratitude

Another staple of topping up your energy accounts is appreciation and gratitude. Some of you are rolling your eyes right now. Bear with me! I get it. I get that the happy-clappy social media crowd are all out there telling you to make everything positive, and sometimes that grates. It feels fake, and I'm the first one to call that out. Here in the Unbreakable office, we shudder at those throw-away fridge magnet 'It's called the present because it's a gift!' style quotes. But, when it comes to recovering and looking after yourselves, appreciation and gratitude are two more heavyweights. There have been many scientific studies on the impact that feeling and expressing gratitude have on the brain. The Mindfulness Awareness Research Centre of UCLA states that gratitude alters the neural structures in the brain, making us feel happier and more content. Feeling grateful and appreciating others when they do something nice for you triggers the good hormones and regulates the effective functioning of the immune system. Neuroscientists and psychologists agree that by activating the brain's reward centre, gratitude exchange alters how you see the world and yourself.

The trouble is, very often, it can feel like you have nothing much to be grateful for. After all, we have been talking about how, when you are burnt out and experiencing low mood you can become cynical, which affects how you think and see the world around you. Something I used to do when I felt I had nothing much to be grateful for was to imagine that I had lost everything I had: my health, the roof over my head, my friends, my family: and I'd really allow myself to feel it. Then I would imagine waking up the next day and it all being back. How grateful I would feel.

That is useful. It's also useful to remember that many of the things around you that you take for granted were once goals, they didn't exist and you made them happen. All these things only lose their spark for one reason. You stopped appreciating them as much. After all, they are easy to appreciate when things are new and novel. We love new and novel things. Our brain pays much more attention and releases the feel-good chemical dopamine when thinking about them. So really, making an effort to appreciate things is a skill.

Meditation

Meditation and breathing are two more incredible things to help us look after ourselves. Meditation can be much more of an awareness-based practice. Simply closing your eyes and becoming aware of your mind, thoughts and feelings. Slowly but surely creating a little distance between your thoughts and that peaceful and restful spot that is your presence.

This book is far from an instruction manual; just know that practising meditation will benefit you in many ways. An interesting finding from research conducted by Yale University found that mindfulness meditation decreases activity in the default mode network (DMN). This is the brain network responsible for mind-wandering and so-called negative thinking, when your mind is simply wandering from thought to thought in an unconstructive way.

As mind-wandering is typically associated with being less happy, ruminating, and worrying about the past and future, it's the goal for many people to dial this down. Several studies have shown that meditation appears to do just this and that even when the mind does wander, meditators are more skilled at bringing it back.

In 2011, Dr Sara Lazar and her team at Harvard found that mindfulness and meditation can change the brain's structure:

> Eight weeks of mindfulness-based stress reduction (MBSR) was found to increase cortical thickness in the hippocampus, which governs learning and memory.

Changes were also seen in some regions of the brain that play a role in emotion regulation and self-referential processing. In addition:

> There were also decreases in brain cell volume in the amygdala, which is responsible for fear, anxiety, and stress – and these changes matched the participants' self-reports of their stress levels, indicating that meditation not only changes the brain, but it changes our subjective perception and feelings as well.

Breathwork

Breathing is a potent tool to improve your energy. The way you breathe is continuously affecting your nervous system. Most of us breathe too shallowly and too much, generally through our mouths. Again, I won't give you a full breakdown of breathing. There are entire books dedicated to that which do a much better job. Just know that the way you breathe drastically impacts your feelings and stress levels.

In general, you will need to breathe more slowly (around one breath per ten seconds), deeper into your belly and chest, through your nose, and ensure the breath out is longer than in. That kind of breath will relax and calm you down. If you can add in this type of breathing throughout the day, say when sitting in the car, before eating or waiting in a queue somewhere you will soon start to see the benefits. If you can get ten breaths like that at a tempo of four seconds in and six seconds out in a relaxed, smooth and steady manner, you will calm down and lower your stress levels throughout the day.

It's helpful to stop thinking of breathing as only something you do when you need it and see it as something that is always happening. If you can set little points in your day when you practise it then you won't end up *needing* to do it as a reaction to feeling rubbish. Of course, you can use millions of other techniques for different results. This one should be a staple for most of us to limit the stress response and stop us from burning out.

Sunlight

Sunshine is another important thing you can get more of to improve your energy throughout the day, particularly first thing in the morning. Sunlight in your eyes when you wake up has been shown to release a healthy cortisol level into your system. That promotes focus and wakefulness throughout your day. On the flip side, the later we get that first dose of sunlight in our eyes the later cortisol gets released, which has been linked to low mood. The other benefit is it gets your natural sleep rhythms kicked off, meaning you will get a better night's sleep. Very often in the winter months, as our natural light is harder to come by, our mood drops.

For many people, using a SAD lamp early in the morning and throughout the day where you are working can improve this dramatically and is something I have found really improves my energy and focus throughout my day.

Nature and novelty

Nature and novelty are two other greatly helpful things for us. Getting outside in nature has been shown to be both soothing and restorative. If you stop to appreciate it, you will get the double whammy of creating what is known as the 'awe effect'. The awe effect can best be described as realising how big the world is and how small you are. It's when you marvel at the stars or get fascinated by something beautiful. Beautiful views are also incredibly calming for our brains: looking out over the sea, across the land, over some hills, across a local park. Visiting beautiful places, getting out in nature and taking it all in are things to consider doing.

Feeding your soul is another great way to top up your accounts. This could be defined as doing things for you, things you enjoy or love, and doing things for others. I can honestly say this may be the easiest part to forget; after all, I'm sure you can find millions of reasons why you can't do things for yourself. It doesn't have to be complicated though. Some favourites of mine are drinking a cup of tea and listening to music, eating my favourite meal, meeting a friend, treating myself to something, reading, and playing the piano. It's all that soulful stuff that goes beyond the physical benefits.

Think of hobbies you may have, those things you love, or even used to love and have stopped doing. What about doing things for others? It's easy for you to think, 'well, I run around after everyone so I am always doing things for others'. It may help to separate what you feel is an obligation, such as looking after kids and work, etc., to truly give to others. Giving should always make us feel good; it should never feel like we are losing something by giving to another human being. It can be compliments, it can be hugs. It can be acts of appreciation, and it can simply be giving what you genuinely value with no need for anything in return, such as stopping to give your time or happiness to people. When filling up your bank accounts, feeding your soul will always go down well and leave you feeling refreshed and recharged.

Sleep

Sleep is an incredibly active process. When sleeping, you consolidate your memory, flush out toxins in your brain, refresh neurons, process stress and repair your brain and body. Poor sleep has been shown to cause serious memory issues. Poor sleep reduces control over unwanted thoughts, increases anxiety disorders and removes your ability to unlearn fear-based memories. Some studies have concluded that there is an increased risk of heart attacks in those who sleep poorly. This is most likely related not only to the poor food choices we all tend to make when we are chronically tired, but also due to the added stress hormones flying about our bodies.

Regard sleep as a massive contribution to recovering as if your life depended on it. With sleep, most experts will say a good seven and a half to eight hours of quality sleep is the gold standard. But in all honesty, if you are struggling to get anywhere near that, just understand that getting just a bit more will help you no end. Again, you can't expect to suddenly find the time to get an 8-hour stretch in every night, but like with everything else, just adding a little more of the good stuff in will help hugely. Some real keys to quality sleep are going to bed and waking up at the same time each day (this may well be the most important to get our rhythms in order). Getting outside when you wake up. Cutting out caffeine after 12-1 pm.

Getting some exercise and activity in throughout the day. Getting off screens before bed. Making your room as cold, dark and quiet as possible and using the bedroom for two things only: sleep and (as my dad would say) 'bonking.' Watching TV or playing on your phone in bed only conditions your brain to see your bed as something you don't go to sleep in. Even more recently, studies have shown that screen time between 11 pm and 4 am activates brain circuits that suppress dopamine (the feel-good hormone). Looking at your screen at night is actively depressing you. So, keep your bedroom for sleeping or having sex.

When it comes to topping up your energy accounts daily all these basics will help. Not only that, they are also pretty much all free. No need for an expensive retreat and no gadgets are required. In most cases, you simply need a pen and a journal; other than that, it's a case of using what you have with a bit more skill than you currently do. Don't underestimate them. They all are proven, and when you stack them up over time, they will help you not only get out of burnout but also to stay out of it. At the end of the chapter, you will get some simple ways to build these into your day-to-day life. Until then, let's see how you can use stress to your advantage.

Stress isn't all that bad, you know

There are two kinds of stress: the type that makes us stronger over time and the type that breaks us down. For example, the stress involved in working towards a meaningful and worthwhile goal can help us grow as individuals, but chronic daily anxiety or stress around our life only breaks us down.

One fantastic way to use and manipulate our stress response to our benefit is to use acute stress as a tool. Acute stress is short-term stress; if you healthily create it yourself, you can use it to reduce long-term, chronic stress and reboot your nervous system.

When I started trying to get myself together, I ended up doing a Wim Hoff course – this was before he was a big deal and all over TV. Back then, I watched him in what looked like his kitchen. He would sit with his dog and play the guitar, and I would listen to him talk about the benefits of the cold and a specific type of rapid breathing. In truth, I was only there because I had been reading about how acute stress (in Wim's case, he uses the cold and his breathing to create this) can reduce chronic stress.

How?

To keep it simple, imagine you have two sides to your nervous system. There is the accelerator that responds to stress. When you get stressed, it gets pushed down and you respond accordingly; you are flushed with stress chemicals and go through the normal human stress response. Now, in a person who's operating well, when the need for that response is over, the other side of our nervous system kicks in, i.e., the brake. The brake stops the reaction and returns us to a normal state.

The trouble with burnout is that the accelerator is stuck down, so our brake stops working. Here is where acute stress comes in. Acute stress puts such short sharp stress on us that the accelerator jams down hard, and all of a sudden, the brake has a significant overreaction; it wakes up and applies itself harder than usual. As a result, chronic stress lowers. Now that is overly simplistic, but you get what I am saying. Acute stress can help lower chronic stress.

Adding in some daily acute stress is crucial to becoming burn-out-proof, restoring your energy and removing your chronic stress. Across our Unbreakable Courses, we encourage people to practise a little deliberate cold exposure, early on. The simplest method is having cold showers.

There are a whole host of benefits to intentional cold exposure, such as the significant release of **epinephrine** (aka adrenaline) and **norepinephrine** (aka noradrenaline) in the brain and body. Cold causes their levels to stay elevated for some time, and their ongoing effect after exposure is an increase in your level of energy and focus.

It's also been shown to release elevated amounts of **dopamine** throughout the day. Dopamine is responsible for drive and feels good, so the result is that you crave less pleasure throughout the day and make better decisions. The other benefit is that it can help you build mental grit because it forces you to exert what is called 'top-down control'. That is when you suppress your reflexive reaction (after all, not many of us want to stand under cold water), so when the inevitable urge to get out shows up in your mind, you control that and stay in there – you build grit. Even better, that grit carries over to other areas of your life and you become better at controlling your stress responses.

Of course, the question is, how cold and how much? Dr Andrew Huberman stated that 11 minutes per week, consisting of two to four sessions of around two to five mins each at an uncomfortably cold temperature, is a great place to start. So, if you have seen people jumping in ice baths all day and think you have to go there for the benefits, you don't. Many people on our courses start with a ten-second blast at the end of their usual shower and work up from there.

The most important thing to remember is that one of the worst things you can do is add more chronic, daily, physical and mental stress to yourself. All that will do is drive you further into running on empty.

When it comes to stress, you either want to add the short sharp stuff, such as cold showers, fast and intense bursts of exercise, or the slow and steady stuff, such as walks or stretching (among other things) all the time, staying out of the middle.

Building in some active recovery and some acute stress is an excellent approach to getting the most out of your energy and feeling as good as possible.

You can change things too, you know

"Grant to us the serenity of mind to accept that which cannot be changed; courage to change that which can be changed, and wisdom to know the one from the other."

Reinhold Niebuhr

Upping your capacity energetically is, of course, the first port of call for you when it comes to feeling better and restoring your energy. From there, you can start to look at the areas in your life outside of you that are causing high-stress levels and ask what you can do about them.

Too often, it's easy to start to work on yourself and hope that everything around you will transform by simply doing that. Some things need changing, and more importantly, you can change some things. You learned about the many triggers that can cause burnout earlier in chapter 4 (See How did we get here? on page 76):

- Lack of control
- Lack of reward
- Lack of community
- Lack of fairness
- Values clashes
- Work overload

It is useful to ask yourself questions at times. Where are these triggers present for you? What are the main issues that cause you worry and concern? What areas of your life are constantly a source of stress? We all have them, and they will change with the ebb and flow of life.

easy to get caught in the trap of managing or coping with them, maybe even tolerating them. That, though, is a surefire way to drain your energy, through the constant daily struggle to manage something that possibly doesn't need to be there after all. So, having the courage to change the things that can be changed is the next step in restoring your energy and really living. It's not easy, though, is it? After all, if it were we would all be doing it.

I have never met anyone in my time coaching or in life who hasn't tried to avoid the discomfort of making the changes they know can be made for the best. That includes me.

After all, it's much easier to avoid the discomfort of change and settle for the discomfort of the situation instead. Some do it for years until they decide, 'now is the time'. I've spoken to many people whose biggest stressor is their lack of money. They often choose to think positively about their lack of cash or work hard dealing with the stress of not having enough, rather than working on solving the problem of not having more of the stuff.

I've met people who have gritted out an unhappy relationship until burnout, rather than putting in the energy into either working on it or leaving it. I've met countless people who have tolerated terrible team members in the workplace instead of embracing the discomfort of moving them on. Guess what? I have been all of those people as well. If you are like me, you may utter the words 'I can't' when changing something or leaving a situation is needed.

In some cases, you are right. There are some things that you cannot undo or change. Very often, though, if you look at things a little more closely, your cant's are carefully disguised wont's. You simply aren't willing to make the changes that are possible.

In my experience, it's much better to admit you aren't willing to do something, than shift the responsibility outside of you and say you can't do something. If anything, it makes accepting where you are much more challenging when you feel you don't have a choice. Acknowledging that you do have a choice and just aren't willing to make that choice is a much more honest outlook to embrace. The admission of this removes the need for the energy it takes to fight your corner in insisting that you can't make the choice. Admitting that you just won't make it actually gives you back a little of your power.

So, addressing the triggers in your life that can be addressed and creating solutions for the problems in your life that can be solved are steps that can free up vast amounts of energy and reduce a whole lot of stress. After all, what you resist will persist and the longer and harder you resist dealing with the things in your life that can be dealt with, the harder they persist and fight back. All that does is take up a tremendous amount of energy, which could be put into creating a better life for yourself. Fighting what you don't want takes just as much energy as building what you do.

Maybe you feel you simply don't have the courage, though? Very often, it's not courage you lack, it's just energy, which is why step one is always to work on your wellbeing and energy. From there, you'll have the raw fuel to deal with the next step.

Maybe you still doubt yourself even then. At that point, you may find it helpful to remind yourself of all the struggles you have previously overcome in your life. Look at all the things you have created and all the solutions you have found. Consider this; rather than not having the courage to change things; you have simply got a little out of practice.

Another thing that may stop you from making changes is a lack of acknowledgement of how staying where you are affects your life. Staying positive about something is great until it leads to trying to 'out-positive' those things which are not helping you. Essentially you are using positivity as an excuse to stay where you are. If you suspect that you may be doing this, it is worth asking yourself a few questions. What has this situation cost you in the past, both personally and in your day-to-day life? What is it costing you now? And even more eye-opening, what will a failure to address it cost you in three to five years? Considering that alone can provide you with the motivation you need to change the things that can be changed.

Or, maybe you just don't want to change. There is nothing wrong with that either, but at least having acknowledged that you are aware of your decision and its potential consequences is important.

So, ask yourself what your most significant stressors are in life. Do you have any control over any of them? If so, what can you do? How about the things you absolutely can't change and have no control over, or the things you have admitted you won't change; and you find the serenity of mind to accept those as they are?

Sometimes it's just the way it is

> "When we are no longer able to change a situation, we are challenged to change ourselves."
>
> Victor Frankl, 'Man's Search for Meaning.'

What about those triggers that can't be changed? What about the stressors in your life that are truly out of your control? At this point, you are left with the task of tackling your perspective of them, and it turns out your perspective is powerful.

Harvard did a study on stress and perspective.

Almost 30,000 participants were monitored in an exploration of how the relationship between the experience of stress and the perception of stress affects health and mortality. The participants were asked two principal questions: how stressful is your life, and do you think stress is good or bad?

The people who said they were quite stressed and thought stress was a negative thing came out lowest on the scale of health markers. They demonstrated earlier indications of developing a higher risk of stress-related illness and premature mortality.

Next in line were the people who said they weren't particularly stressed at that time, but that stress was a bad thing which negatively impacts life. They also came out worse on the scale of suffering than people who said they had a stressful life but felt stress could be positive.

The clever people at Harvard proposed the theory that *the way you choose to perceive stress in itself can have a significant influence on how it affects you mentally and physically.* Does that mean you should just tolerate these stressful things and tell yourself they are good? I don't think so. It goes back to the meaning that you attribute to stress. Just like the meaning you give to incidents in your past, your perception is everything, and your perception of something can be directed or chosen by you. This is where asking yourself good solid questions can make all the difference.

"Am I looking at what is right or what is wrong here?"

"Am I focused on what I can't do or what I can?"

"How could I look at this in a way that could help me move forwards?"

What's the best outcome that I can work towards here? These simple questions can help you regain some control over your perspective if you write them down.

Of course, very often, life comes along and lifes you, and no amount of questions can seem to alter your perspective.

You may all feel the regret and remorse of decisions made or not made and know that you cannot undo those things, however much you would like to. Many people experience loss and devastation in their life through no doing of their own. 'Why me? Why now?" What are you left with in those situations? You are tasked with the difficult challenge of accepting. Yet accepting can seem passive, as if you are rolling over and quitting. Acceptance can feel like giving up or taking the easy way out. Anyone who has faced up to issues in life, stood face to face with pain and hurt or stress and worry, looked them in the eye and said 'OK, this is how it is', will tell you it's far from rolling over and giving up.

Acceptance is having the courage to face things as they are and embrace what you truly don't want to. It's not to be confused with consenting or agreeing, either. Accepting how you feel about something does not mean you agree with it as a 'good thing'. You are simply saying, 'OK, this is how it is'.

Accepting the situation as it is, opens up the opportunity to choose what it can mean for you. There is great freedom in selecting the meaning of life's events for yourself. Without acceptance, you will stay stuck in a battle to change what you know deep down you can't.

Maybe that is where you can start to understand what Victor Frankl meant by:

> "In some ways suffering ceases to be suffering at the moment it finds a meaning, such as the meaning of a sacrifice."

Finding meaning in pain is *not* finding the good in a bad situation. Sometimes there is no 'good' to be found. Instead, 'so what does this mean for me and my life now?'

To take charge of your perspective, to gain a complete understanding of what you cannot change, and to find meaning in the hurt you may be experiencing is a difficult task. It calls upon you to be patient and compassionate with yourself, to be greater than your current reality. In some cases, you may be able to do this quite quickly; in others, you may go back and forth with it for a while.

Just remember, in finding some kind of meaning for yourself, you can start to feel greater and avoid the burnout that comes with fighting against what you can't control.

Try this

It's time to put what you have just read into practice. The following steps are great ways to start topping up your energy and feeling calmer, energised and mentally fresher. As always, some things will require a pen and paper. The first step you can do right away. The others are simple routines you can plug into your day.

Step 1: Get calmer right now

A. Set a timer for three to five minutes and note how you feel right now.

B. Take a relaxed breath through your nose, deep into your belly but don't force it; let it feel easy, don't try to make it longer than you need to, and close your eyes if it's appropriate and safe.

C. Let out a more extended breath, like you are blowing on hot soup. Again, nice and steady. The key is to make the out-breath longer than your in-breath but still slow and steady.

D. Keep repeating this, remaining nice, slow and steady with your breath, always keeping the out-breath longer than your in-breath.

E. When the timer goes off, note that you feel slightly calmer as this helps you anchor it into your day.

Step 2: Night-Time primer

A. Set an alarm for 30 minutes before you want to go to bed. That signals your bedtime. When that alarm goes off, no matter what you are doing, go to bed and stop using all media, including your phone.

B. Have a hot bath or shower.

C. Grab a journal and write down 3-5 things you have to be grateful for from today or your life as a whole.

D. Practise the breathing exercise, from step 1, in bed for 5-10 minutes.

Step 3: Morning primer

A. Drink a small glass of water as soon as you wake up and get outside for a few minutes at least.

B. Set a timer for four minutes and move. Dance, jog on the spot, whatever. Just get moving.

C. Practise the breathing exercise from step 1 for eight to ten minutes.

D. Finish your shower with a blast of the cold for twenty to thirty seconds to get all the benefits of the cold exposure we spoke about earlier.

Step 4: Reframe your stress

A. Write down the stuff that's stressing you.

B. Circle what you can control

C. Ask what you can do for each one of the things you can control right now.

D. Pick one and do it right now.

E. Schedule another one for tomorrow.

The rituals and tasks on this page are simple ways to start topping up your energy accounts, recover more effectively so you can restore your energy and use acute stress in useful ways. The next step on our path is to look at what's going on inside that skull of yours and give you some insights and skills to make it work for you, not against you.

A quick recap

Burnout is not 'normal' or 'just a part of life'. Continually replenishing your energy accounts is vital when it comes to mitigating the effects of burnout.

1. There are two forms of recovery. Active and Passive. Active recovery is vital if you want healthy levels of well-being. Prioritise active recovery into your life as much as you can.

2. You have three bank accounts: physical, mental and emotional. Topping these up daily with small investments is vital if you want to feel greater.

3. Short, sharp, acute stress such as cold water therapy, is incredibly good for your nervous system. Consider starting with up to 11 mins per week with a temperature that is uncomfortably cold for you.

4. Change the things you can change. You will waste vast amounts of energy and end up burnt out if you keep avoiding and tolerating the things that cause stress in your life when you could change them.

5. Not all stressors in your life can be changed. At this point, your power lies in finding the most helpful meaning for you and your future. Acceptance is the first step towards this. Fighting against what you can't change will burn you out down the line.

PART 3

Think Greater...

6

STOP FIGHTING START TRAINING

Let's start off with a little story with a big lesson:

> I was sitting in a beautiful living room a few months back, looking at a picture of a lady called Parashanti; the mother-in-law of my good friend and meditation teacher, Arjuna Ishaya.
>
> Seeing that photograph transported me back to around eight years earlier. I was in a dark and chilly office in South Shields with a group of men, and we were a day and a half into a coaching experience. Like most of the men there, I had come to get more out of my life and make some sense of myself and my behaviour. To be blunt, I was there to try and sort my shit out.

Minds can be strange companions, chattering away at us; some of it great, some of it awful. Back then, most of my internal chatter was awful. I hated my mind, which was full of criticism, doubt, self-loathing, anxiety and anger. Like many of us, the trouble is that I was living in it constantly. I spent my days doing what much of the self-help advice I'd tried implementing suggested I do: arguing with it, distracting it, out-talking it, really just plain old fighting it in the hope it would shut up. The thing is, as we all know, what we continue to fight rarely shuts up. Constant sparring with your mind only serves to create an even more skilled opponent.

As Einstein said (and I'll paraphrase him here), peace cannot be kept by force, only understanding. The thing is, I couldn't understand my brain at all. After all, who teaches us that? So, there I sat in South Shields, waiting for a monk to walk in and talk about meditation. I was, of course, keen to hear what would be said, but at the same time I was a little sceptical.

Then, as Parashanti came floating through the middle of the rows of chairs where we, a group of cold, anxious men, were all sitting, a big smile across her face, it became obvious that she had something about her.

The room was mesmerised by her presence; a gentle, relaxed, yet confident energy radiated from her. Over a few hours, she taught us about thoughts and meditation, introducing us to some concepts and then backing them up with a little practicality. She spoke about how we all spend a lot of time wrestling with our thoughts, and yet we aren't our thoughts.

We aren't our thoughts. How many times do you hear that phrase peddled by people? As if it's that easy. It's one thing to want to believe it, but another to truly know it. That day I had my first glimpse of that feeling as she guided us through exercise after exercise. For the first time in as long as I could remember, I observed my thoughts through a lens of compassion and curiosity, watching them as if they were passing visitors. I felt a sense of calm and peace. If I could pick a defining moment from when training my thoughts, then it was that moment. We can glimpse what is possible when we have the skill and grace to observe and understand our minds.

I realised for the first time I had been playing the wrong game. I had spent years trying to shut my mind up, muzzle it, distract it, and at times sedate it in an effort to find peace. Yet, all that did was strengthen the resolve of those thoughts which kept them coming back stronger.

As Arjuna walked back into that sitting room I was smiling, looking at the photo. He knew what I was smiling about for sure. Parashanti died soon after that day in South Shields; she had terminal cancer. Those four hours gave me hope. They gave me something to reach for; the knowledge that I could be rid of that inner turmoil and live freely. They were a catalyst to go and explore all I could when it came to how our brains operate, from the science to the spiritual, to understand, train and stop fighting. Since then, Unbreakable has helped thousands of people develop a mind that works for them rather than against them.

In helping me experience a sense of peace for a few hours, Parashanti has indirectly helped thousands of you. I remain ever grateful for that meeting.

We don't see the world as it is, we see it as we are

If fighting your mind isn't helping, the answer is to start to understand, train and work with it. The question is, how do you train it and have mastery over how you experience the day-today moments of your lives? Let's start with how the brain deals with the world which is on the outside of you.

The smallest unit of measurement used for measuring data is a bit. eight bits of data make a byte (think of the kilobytes, megabytes and gigabytes available on your computer.) Mihaly Csikszentmihalyi estimated that we can hold about 120 bits of information per second in our conscious attention. This isn't that much considering that the brain is exposed to around a million bits per second. So, your brain is locked away in your skull, trying to figure out what to pay attention to and what not to pay attention to. What is essential information, and what isn't? Your brain is filtering those million bits of information into roughly 120 bits and, as it does, creating much of how we experience the day-to-day moments of our lives. So, the question now becomes, what are you paying attention to and why? Attention is a complex thing. I will save you a neuroscience lecture and not turn this into a hard-to-read boredom-fest.

In a nutshell, neither your brain nor anyone's brain, could handle processing one million bits of information and trying would take far too much energy. Therefore, you evolved to filter the reality around you, to place your attention only on that which you feel is important.

There are three common ways that you filter incoming information. Firstly, there is how you feel. Everyone has felt very sad, upset or hurt, and have you noticed how when you are experiencing sadness, you suddenly seem to be hyper-alert to sadness? You pick up on all that is sad around you. You hear sad music everywhere and mournful, heart-rending lyrics jump out at you. Similarly, you will be feeling great, and suddenly, everything seems to be working out for you. Even the tough parts of your day don't seem so challenging. Likewise, you can scroll through social media in a bad mood and find things that support that. You can feel rubbish and while having a conversation with someone take what they say the wrong way, picking up on the slightest bit of negativity.

How you feel dictates much of the information that comes to your attention. We covered burnout and restoring your energy for a whole two chapters because how you feel hugely affects what you focus on and think about. Then there is past experience. The brain is not recording reality around us. It is constructing reality based upon everything you have learned or experienced up until that very point in time. Now, that may sound a bit mad, but I am not getting all philosophical here and asking 'does anything really exist?' I am pointing out that at every moment you are alive, your brain is taking in the data around you and comparing it to all of the similar past experiences you have had before. It's a miraculous thing. Your brain is continuously analysing the data that enters it via your senses. Using all that information, it constructs what it believes to be 'true', based on the library of stored information that it has to hand. However, as we know, the brain loves shortcuts and gets things wrong sometimes.

This 'getting it wrong', well, we all know how that pans out in life. Your past experiences, especially negative ones, cause you to anticipate those scenarios cropping up again. If you have had a panic attack in a coffee shop and you walk into another one, your brain reminds you of that and suddenly, you are hyperaware and on the precipice of panicking once again. Past experiences have a considerable influence on how you perceive the reality around you and once you know that you can see how important it is to learn to remember better memories. You will have had some great past experiences. One of the brilliant things I have learnt in my time coaching, is that when people start to progress, they always comment on how they begin to remember great memories that they had forgotten.

The other way you are filtering those 120 bits of information per second, that make up your life experience, is what you are choosing to pay attention to. For example, you are choosing to read this book right now, so you are paying attention to it; if something grabs your attention outside these pages, you may look to see what it is. There is a part of your attention system called the 'central executive' that says 'hang on a minute, we are meant to be reading the book,' so it adjusts your behaviour, and you return to the task at hand. If you didn't have that bit working, you would never pay attention to what you decided was important. That part also works on goals and intentions. Imagine for a second that you wake up and think, 'Today is going to be awful!' and give that thought lots of energy for a few minutes. Well, through the process of letting that idea settle and take root, it, ironically and unintentionally, becomes an intention. So, as you go about your day you filter more data from outside of yourself to back up that intention.

Or, if you decide you want a particular car and start looking at them online and researching them, you will notice that you start seeing more of them on the roads around you. Your brain thinks they are now important and so highlights them around you. Now you know why the first part of this book was geared around deciding what is important to you and reminding you not to let your spark go out. Intentions and goals are powerful ways in which you filter the world around you to create your experience of it.

There are many more ways that the brain seeks to filter and construct our reality. This isn't a deep dive into the brain; however, the mission statement of this book is to give you the right step at the right time and those three areas of our brain's 'filtration system' are the three principal ones we will break down further throughout this chapter for you.

All in all, you see the world through your unique lens, garnering information based on what you expect, how you feel and what's happened to you in the past. When you understand this, you can stop fighting against your patterns and start to use skills to improve those filters. That's when life can really begin to move in the direction you want.

What about that inner chatter?

The world around us is one thing, but what about that most tricky and complicated of areas – the world within us? As much as your attention is filtering what is outside of you, often your attention is very much focused upon what is happening inside you. We all focus on the thoughts and feelings of our inner world a great deal. We use our imagination to worry about things that haven't yet happened and create fearful future scenarios for ourselves. We use our memory to go over a painful past and relive things that make us feel pain or sadness, shame or guilt. In turn, that too, creates the experience of our life. Our inner and outer worlds are undoubtedly linked in an eternal dance of creation and experience. So how can you create some mastery over your inner world? How can you start to take control of how you feel, worry less and live more? In much the same way your focus works on the outside of you, it also works that way inside you.

The mind mansion is an analogy I first heard about from Dandapani a Sikh monk. I've tweaked it over the years into our own Unbreakable version, and if you can grasp it, you will start to see how you can train your attention in that mind of yours and become mentally free of many of the things that hold you back.

Imagine for a moment that your mind is a big mansion with many rooms. (Prepare yourself; you will see the words 'mind mansion' a lot in the following pages!)

In your mansion, you have rooms for the past and rooms for the future. These can be happy rooms, sad rooms, anxious rooms, and loving rooms. Your mind mansion and the rooms within it are static; they don't move anywhere. You travel around that mansion, and as you do, you open doors to the many rooms, sit in them, and experience each one.

You may be drinking your morning tea, and your mind is static, but you have travelled to the 'future room' in your mind mansion. Or if you are worrying you are in the 'worry room', and when you are in there, you experience worry. Then you may wander across your mind mansion to a 'past room', where you sit surrounded by all the thoughts of your past. You feel disappointed about a mistake you made, and while you are drinking your tea, you can't leave the 'disappointed room' in your mind. You jump in the car in the real, physical world, but you are still in that room in your mind. You go to work and are still there. The longer you stay in that room, the stronger it becomes. Now that room is effortless to go to, you have been doing it every day for years — so the room becomes a habit and harder, as time goes on, to get out of.

We all have rooms in our mind mansion that are easy to go to and some that we would rather not go to. Some are simply open because we keep going there and it's a habit. Some are open because something happened, and when that thing happened, it pushed us into that room with extreme energy, and the room is now so strong we find it hard not to be pulled in there over and over again.

The key thing to understand here is that what is moving around your mind mansion is you; you are moving your attention around it. I can move your attention right now by asking you to remember a really happy time in your life. Who was there? What was happening? What were you wearing? What could you hear? Did you eat? Did you have a drink? The more I ask these questions, the more I get you to move your attention through your mind to find those answers. It is important to grasp that your mind is static, and you are moving your attention and focus through it. See what I am saying here?

When you realise that, you can start to understand that many of the methods we are taught to use aren't training our attention. They are asking us to fight our minds. Trying to think positively when you are anxious is, basically, sitting in the anxiety room of your mind mansion and trying to out-think it from inside that room. But you are still in there. You can say you aren't anxious all you like, but you're still in that room of your mind mansion. You can try and destroy the rooms you don't like in your mansion, but that never works, and they stubbornly stay intact. All that energy you used to go into that room and destroy it has only made that room stronger.

The trouble with all those other methods is that it takes enormous energy to distract yourself and this, eventually, leads to so much fatigue that your attention runs wild anyway. The best solution is to train your attention and focus so that it is under your command. To create a mind mansion where no room is off limits because all rooms serve a purpose. To simply know what room you are in, have the ability to move to the ones that serve you and at the same time step out of the ones that no longer do. Of course, that isn't easy, and many things will make it difficult for you to navigate your mind.

Just know that the first step is always understanding how it works because then you can start to work with your mind, not against it.

It's not your fault you suck at it

Of course, as I said, this is a challenge. We are bombarded with daily reminders to 'just' be present, 'just' practise being mindful, 'just' eat less, let go, think positive or 'just' appreciate what you have. It's incredible how so many of the things that have 'just' in front of them are usually extremely hard to do. Why is it so hard to 'just' think positive or train your attention to focus on the useful things in your life?

Well, for starters, you live in a world of distraction with your attention being bombarded from every angle with things that want to hijack it away from you. Your phone pings with instant messages, notifications, calls and emails. The news comes faster and is more visually impactful to you than ever before. Social media is designed in such a way as to keep you on it for as long as possible.

These things are so easy to get distracted by because they are novel, and the brain loves novelty. They also release large amounts of dopamine into your brain. When that notification goes off and you get some love, you feel good and you release dopamine. That dopamine tells you that whatever triggered its release makes you feel good, so you focus more on that trigger in the future.

Dopamine is your brain's chief reward chemical. It's also your number one focusing chemical. This means whatever you deem to be fuelling you with more of it, becomes easier to pay attention to. This is why we all find social media an easy time warp, where hours can pass without us noticing. It is also why that little red number denoting messages and notifications is so hard to ignore. We want to experience the potential dopamine hit at the other end of that 'ping'.

So, you have your inner world where a bad night's sleep and some poor food can lessen your ability to focus your attention. In addition, it is where the past events of your life play out in emotionally charged memories, hurt, pain, people and places lost. Then you have the outside world where external outfits like the media and advertising industries know all too well what will draw your attention.

Fear is a big hitter, and fear-inducing headlines and clickbait are everywhere. The word 'industry' here is the operative one. It is essential to be aware that your attention is a commodity – a valuable commodity which is ultimately worth a great deal of money. Human attention and focus are now worth billions, and yours are no different.

Now here is the big question, the very reason that Unbreakable exists today... Did anyone ever teach you to focus? When did you learn the practical skills to focus on valuable things that help and don't hinder you?

To get anywhere near the life you desire, it is essential to recognise the necessity of learning these skills. You may think that it is universally recognised that we humans benefit from being 'mindful' that is all it is: a recognition of what we need to work on without practical advice on how to do that.

Instead of practical and valuable skills training, you are bombarded with nice sayings, lovely bumper-sticker quotes, a vague awareness of what might help and half-hearted reminders that 'what we focus on grows'. You are not given any actual practical steps to either implement such philosophies or action them.

To keep us safe, our attention is built to wander, to look ahead, behind and all around. Part of the function of our attention is to be distracted by potential danger. If our prehistoric ancestors focussed on only one thing in front of them, they would miss the predator sneaking up behind them, ready to take them out. Add to that the plethora of things that you get taught by so many in the personal development industry; it is no wonder that you find that training your attention becomes harder.

I say all this so that you can give yourself a break when you struggle to keep your attention on the useful things in your life. None of us is immune to our attention getting the better of us. Attention is something that monks may dedicate their whole life to training, yet here we are hoping to gain monk-like focus by following one breathing audio and a TikTok on mindfulness.

Don't beat yourself up when your attention gets pulled in an unhelpful direction. Remind yourself that you are a work in progress, and remind yourself that all you can do is the best you can with what you have. Some days you will be tired, and some days life will life you, so brush yourself off and go again, because your attention is always working somehow. Making an effort to make it work in your favour will never be a wasted effort, even on the off days.

Train like a Jedi master

This wouldn't be an Unbreakable book if I didn't reference Star Wars. I apologise if you aren't into it (— seriously, why aren't you into it!?) But it's time to let you know that the Unbreakable Office deeply respects the battle between light and dark within all those characters from a long time ago, in that galaxy far away.

None of them is all good, and none all bad. Even Darth Vader (who you *must* have heard of, surely?) has elements of 'good' within him. Poor Vader is the product, you could say, of setting up camp in the less useful rooms of his mind mansion for very extended periods.

Anyway, back to business and an analogy most of you will get on board with.

There are three keys to training our focus. Keys best summed up in describing a typical walk with my cocker spaniel, Milo. When I first rescued Milo, he was around 12 months old, had no real training and had spent his first year with a lady in her 80s who simply couldn't handle him. He soon sparked to life when he moved with me to the countryside.

I remember my first walks with him. When I let him off the lead he ran everywhere, nose down, picking up scents, moving pheasants along, chasing rabbits, going nuts. The only trouble was he never came back. He had a mind of his own and a bit of a liking for chasing joggers. Living in the Malvern Hills, you see a fair few runners, and before you knew it, he would be jumping up at them wanting to play. Some took it OK, some not, as you can imagine. So, there he would be, trying to lick a runner to death while I was pulling all the usual tricks out of my bag. If you have a dog, you know the ones: pretending I was going, pretending I had food, using my deep, stern voice, using my high-pitched crazy sounding voice, all to no avail. Milo came back when Milo wanted. It was soon apparent that Milo had no training, and he needed some.

If you imagine Milo is your attention for a moment, you can see that a walk with Milo sums up a day in many minds. Our attention is doing what it wants, distracted by anything and everything and causing chaos throughout our mind mansion. I know that is how my early days felt when I started trying to get myself sorted. All because I had no training.

So, what does this training look like, and how do you train your attention?

Let's go for another walk with Milo. Imagine Milo is your attention and you let it off the lead; it runs off doing its thing. The first thing you have to know is Milo's location. You have to know where your attention is. We all like to think that we always know where our attention is, but we often have no idea. So, step one is getting awareness of where your attention is. Once you have done that, you have to get Milo back to where you want him.

Much like your attention, if you know where it is and what room of your mind mansion you are in, you can now learn to move it to a better room, one you want to be in. That is called willpower. In the Unbreakable definition, willpower is not your ability to tolerate where your attention is; it's the mental strength you have to move it to a room that serves you better.

What about when you have Milo where you want him? He's come back, great. Now you want him to stay with you for a little bit. When it comes to keeping attention, that is concentration. When I talk about concentration here, I am talking about having the ability to concentrate and hold your focus where you want it until you choose to move it. This takes skill and practice.

Awareness of your attention and keeping it is the mastery we are looking for. To stay focussed on the things in your life that are important to you, and having the skill to manage your attention gives you the ability to take yourself out of the fearful future and into an exciting one, to step out of a painful past and into the present moment. Even more exciting, you have the power to do it. You do. It's all trainable. Much like Milo, you simply need the right training and practise to start feeling like you are in charge of what goes on, rather than feeling like you are a puppet on a string.

Awareness, willpower, and concentration are what we call the Unbreakable Focus Stack. There are loads of ways to train these three things. Skills such as journalling, breathing and meditation are all great tools to assist you in shifting your awareness and holding it in a better place.

Alongside using those tools, it is useful to practise these skills in day-to-day life, picking the activities you already do and using the Focus Stack. Having a cup of tea/coffee every morning is an ideal time to train your Focus. How? You could start by paying close attention to what you are doing and taking care of each part of the process. If your attention wanders off to what you think you should be doing later, take a breath, notice and bring it back to the tea making. As you drink it, if you notice you want to flick through your phone, again notice this and come back to drinking your tea. It will blow your mind how, when you start becoming aware, just how much your attention is on the lookout for something, how it's always looking to be distracted. You may think you are rubbish at it if your attention keeps wandering off, but this is absolutely not the case! It is not how often your attention wanders off that is the test. It's a fact you have become aware of, used your willpower to bring it back and then started to concentrate again; that is what we are looking for.

You can also train your willpower by picking a task in your day, doing it the best you can, finishing it and then asking how you can do a little more. You will be amazed how often you leave things unfinished in your day, be it your clothes not put away, your desk not tidied, or your washing up not done. We can all be a bit half-assed about stuff. I know I can for sure.

You will be equally amazed at how much you go through the motions when you aren't aware. You may wonder what the big deal is. Well, the big deal is the more you do that throughout your day, the more you are training your attention to do its own thing and the more you do that the less control you will have over it. When you overthink something, you will struggle to bring your attention away from it. When you get caught up in the 'what ifs of life' you will struggle to bring yourself back to something more positive, and maybe even worse, when you are with the people you care about or working on something important, you will lose the ability to keep your attention on it at all. How many moments of your life do you miss, because even though you are physically there, mentally, you are somewhere else?

When I teach concepts like this, people immediately think they must do this all day. Believe me – you won't be able to. I made that mistake and ended up exhausted and frustrated. You simply need to pick something, one thing you do each day and use it to train your focus. Pick a person you see each day and just attempt to focus on them, noting when you are thinking about something else, not listening or being distracted and then simply bring your attention back to them. Not only is that training your focus, but it's also improving the quality of that connection.

The more you train your focus in your day, the more that pays off in dealing with things like your anxiety. If you train yourself to focus only when you need it, for example, when you feel anxious or afraid, you will always find you can't do it. However, if you have been practising most days, when the need of the moment strikes you will rise to it comfortably.

So, in a nutshell, when it comes to your attention, it is no different to training an unruly dog. Like my Milo, you will have days where your attention is playing ball and other days where you have to work slightly harder than you would like. The good news is, it's all about training and everybody can learn and practise no matter who you are or what you have been through. As the Greek poet Archilochus said:

> "We don't rise to the level of our expectations; we fall to the level of our training."

Try this

The following steps are simple ways to train your mind rather than work against it. You will need a pen and paper for step 3. Remember to be patient with the following steps. You won't always find them easy, but that doesn't mean they aren't working. So, make an effort to give yourself a break and be curious about the process of it.

Step 1: Become the observer, Parashanti Style

A. Set a timer for two minutes.

B. Close your eyes and follow your breath, nice and steady, as you learnt in the energy section

C. Notice when you think and count each thought you have. Stay nice and relaxed and breathe naturally. Simply count and add up your thoughts each time you notice you are thinking.

D. After you have noticed you are thinking, return to focusing on your breathing again.

Congratulations, you just observed your thoughts and created some separation. After all, you wouldn't be able to count them if you weren't observing them.

Step 2: Start to focus

A. Tomorrow morning, either make your bed or focus on your shower.

B. Whilst doing the task you chose, try to do it with the best attention to detail you can. Pay attention to really doing the task with as much focus as possible. Feel the physical sensations as much as you can.

C. Notice when your mind wanders off and get back to the task at hand - it doesn't matter that you have forgotten to concentrate. It's great you noticed and brought your focus back.

D. If you get distracted, take a deep breath and simply say the word 'focus' to remind yourself and bring yourself back.

Step 3: Alphabet task

A. Write each letter of the alphabet down the side of a page.

B. Work through the letters finding something starting with each letter that makes you happy, or could make you happy.

C. Feel free to change the aim each time, so instead of happiness, you could list things that make you feel grateful, excited, calm, etc.

D. If you get stuck, move on and return to the task before bed.

The tasks above are simple ways to get started with training your focus.

Next, we will look at the other side of focus and the mind mansion, the parts of the mind mansion you may not like at all. The greater our skill level in dealing with them, the greater our focus will become. If there is any step I need to include in training your mind, this is the biggest.

A quick recap

Rather than fighting your mind through distraction and magical thinking, train it through understanding and practise.

1. You are exposed to a million bits of data a moment and can hold roughly 120-180 in your conscious experience. That 180 makes up your life experience. You can decide what to let in more consistently by training your attention. Fighting against what's in the 180 bits will never work, but manipulating what you give your attention to will.

2. Your attention is built to wander. Your power lies in noticing when it has wandered and bringing it back to where you want it, rather than never letting it wander at all.

3. Three keys to training your attention are awareness, willpower and concentration. Like walking a dog, you can train these skills to improve.

4. Train your attention through small tasks. During your day aim to do one thing only, aim to do it better and with more focus than you usually do. The more you train your attention, the more control you will have over it.

7

MAKING FRIENDS
WITH THE ENEMY

The mind mansion is an analogy that I use repeatedly, and every time it helps people make sense of how their attention works. Whenever I share it, I often hear variations of the same take on it: 'I need to move house!', 'My mind needs some of these rooms blocked up.', 'How can I get rid of some of these rooms?' or 'I need an extension!'

At some point, you learnt that some emotions and behaviours were bad. You learnt to fear them, feel shame about them and feel embarrassed of them. You tried to block them out, conversely giving them more power over you than necessary. Your fear of entering those rooms only keeps you visiting them over and over, when you least want to. Anyone who has studied psychology or media and advertising knows people are drawn to what upsets them, not the opposite.

Seek to understand those rooms and begin to make friends with those parts of yourself that you have deemed 'bad'. You cannot, after all, expect to experience a sense of peace, happiness or calm whilst battling a mind of which you are afraid. You do not have to destroy the elements of yourself that you don't like to become worthy of anything.

Ultimately, you will have to face these emotions head-on anyway. Life will do its thing, and you will experience hurt, pain, and anger at some point. Shitty things will happen. To navigate life's inevitable tests, facing them with less fear will serve you much better. If you have done your darndest to suppress all negativity, all so-called 'bad' human traits, then when they come up and slap you in the face you will be less equipped to deal with them. If you have accepted them as a part of life, you can navigate those times, approach them with compassion and express how you feel. If, on the other hand, you haven't then there is a good chance you will suppress how you feel, try to run away from it and, in turn, stay stuck there.

I spent years trying to destroy the elements of myself I didn't like, trying not to be something or someone. It was exhausting. Not feeling at peace with who you are is not an uncommon thing. It's also not a nice thing. It feels like you have to hide who you are and that you are unworthy of love, happiness and joy, because you aren't a good person deep down. After all, how can you be? You have these parts of yourself that are unlovable, wrong, and undeserving. So, you keep attempting to prove your worth, to prove that you are some things and not others. You try to prove it to yourself and you try to prove it to others. However, no matter how much you prove it is never enough because you have nothing to prove, just things to accept and understand.

Imagine, for a moment, that you have the most incredible mansion, not a mind mansion but an actual mansion. You have many rooms decorated precisely how you want; you love them all. Some are brash, some are calming and relaxed, some busy, some loud and some clean and minimalist, all with different styles you have created and love. You are so proud of it that you have started inviting people over. People, being people, give you their opinions on the rooms. Some of those rooms, they say, are too loud, so you shut the doors and you stop going in them. Some other person describes a room as too dull for their taste, so you shut that door too. Bit by bit, guest by guest, you close rooms up until one room is left that is now acceptable to everyone. The big mansion you loved and created with all your effort and heart is currently limited to one room.

Life is the same. You will allow others to tell you that you are too much of some things and not enough of others and so you learn to shut down the room in your mind that you think is unacceptable. You learn that anxiety or anger are bad things, so you become afraid of those rooms and try to block them out. You get told you are too confident and arrogant, so you stop being proud of yourself. Bit by bit, you not only lose who you are, but you also create another problem. It takes a lot of energy to hide the bits of you that you don't think others like, and it takes a lot of energy to try not to be the bits of you that you don't like. Focus works very much as a two-pronged approach. You spend lots of energy trying to pay attention to what you want to focus on, and in the meantime, you also spend lots of energy trying to block out what you don't.

So, you can imagine how much energy you spend trying to block out everything you think you shouldn't be or would rather not be. Does this mean you should indulge in all life's 'bad' behaviours and actions? That you should be rude and obnoxious and generally repellent? Of course not. It's simply honouring that those parts exist in you and exist in all of us. By seeking to understand those parts of yourself, you can have much more mastery of them.

You may not want to be angry, or you may not like being anxious, but the more you try to suppress those things, the more you try and block those rooms up in your mind mansion, the more energy you expend. Much like holding a beach ball underwater, you can only hold it for so long until it blows up in your face. After all, how often do you become even more anxious while trying to suppress your anxiety? How many times have you got angry with yourself about your anger? By doing everything in your power to deny those parts of yourself, you very often become consumed by that which you want to deny. The more fear you have around experiencing a room of your mind, the more it will dominate your day-to-day life. After all, how often does fear of experiencing anxiety cause you to avoid any situation that might make you uncomfortable? How often does feeling bad about getting angry stop someone from sticking up for themselves? You can look at every room of your mind mansion that you try hard not to be or to experience and see in some way that the fear of it governs your life more than the room itself.

It is helpful to think of everything on a sliding scale. For example, when anxiety is too extreme it can impact your life in so many limiting ways. Still, slight anxiety over something new can keep you engaged and paying attention and help you perform well. Anger at its worst can be destructive and abusive, but at its most useful, it can mean that you stick up for yourself in a healthy way. If people didn't get angry over injustice our society would be very different and repressive.

Honour, but don't indulge

"Your problem is you think you are a piece of shit. I can see it; you hate yourself and feel like you need to be punished for everything you have done wrong. You want to hurt yourself for the hurt you've caused. That is what you are struggling with, and you need to let it go."

Mark Whitehand

Mark said that to me in 2014. It was at that same event that I met Parashanti. Mark was there to document and record the event, but being an incredible coach, mentor and guide, he had a moment where he asked if he could add to the proceedings and enlighten us about what he was seeing. With our permission, he went around the room and broke down, very simply, what he felt was going on for each individual who had come there that day. On reflection, it was a masterful bit of coaching. He had everyone's number that day, and it opened up a new opportunity for me; I could change if I only stopped believing some of the things that kept me stuck.

You are always creating beliefs and identities for yourself. It's one thing to do something terrible, and it's another to label yourself as a terrible person. One is an action, a fuck up, a mistake, and the other is a state of being, a definition of yourself. 'I failed' differs from 'I am a failure.' The latter is self-defining and will determine your view of yourself and how you act from there. The statement 'I am' may be the most powerful statement you can ever make. 'That's just the way I am' is something I often hear from people to back up their mistakes or their struggles. If that is how you see yourself, that is who you will always be. Your actions will reflect the identity you have created for yourself, and so too will the life you experience. What is the truth of who you are? The fact is that you can choose your reality as you move through life. You can decide how you define yourself, and the truth of that will set you free.

Of course, it's very easy to go and indulge those bits of yourself you would rather not be, and this is where you need to be mindful. One can start to think, 'Oh well, this is who I am.' By suggesting that you change the pattern of feeling shame, guilt and self-pity for your past actions, I am not saying you can simply go to town with the 'This is who I am' and put it out there for the world to take it or leave it. Looking at those areas of yourself and simply letting rip is, paradoxically, just as much of an avoidance of facing them as slamming that mind mansion room shut and barricading it. Throwing those parts of yourself out into the world and declaring, 'This is just how I am' and that the world at large can like it or lump it is an excellent way of not looking at those parts of you and not taking responsibility for the impact your actions have upon others.

Not using some emotional intelligence and being aware of how that expression may be unhealthy and un-useful to yourself and others is equally as damaging as trying to block it out.

So, it takes skill and practice to balance your honour and recognition of your so-called 'bad' parts with not indulging them so much that it becomes counterproductive for yourself and your relationships with others. You need to be a bit of a grown-up about it, and that's hard. That's where it takes work. I have both fought my demons and indulged them to the detriment of myself and the people I care about.

The day Mark looked at me directly and let me see what was going on, I was awash with the indulgence of self-pity. Years later, I was indulging with a lack of responsibility. I was in 'Fuck it!' mode. It took a long time for me to realise that honouring those parts of me that I found uncomfortable was different. Honouring comes from acceptance and recognition that you can be and have been these things, yet you are not just these things; they don't define you.

You get to choose how you display the facets of yourself. You are not only anxiety or anger, for example, but you will 100% experience anxiety and anger. It is vital to know that doesn't make you a bad person; it makes you human. With skill, grace and a dose of being less shit, you can understand, accept and embrace the totality of being a human being. With that acceptance and a dose of emotional maturity, you can and will experience mental freedom and choice.

How we avoid honouring the 'bad' bits

It may seem like honouring those rooms of your mind mansion that you don't like is hard work. And you are right. It is. However, as I outlined in the previous chapter, it is much harder, in the long run, to ignore them and try to avoid them or to throw those doors wide open and let the contents run riot. Doing either of these things is a surefire way to let our 'bad' bits affect our lives in ways that hinder us. If honouring them allows us to experience mental and emotional freedom, then avoiding them creates the opposite. It creates fear and discomfort.

Many of us often get into self-help/personal development to try and escape the prison that is our life. We want to get everything fixed. We want to arrange everything how we want it to be. In doing so, we believe that our minds can be filled with the so-called good stuff. The trouble is, in doing this, we very often learn to fear the so-called bad stuff.

So many people are stressed, burnt-out, anxious, over-whelmed and scared of being those things, which is a new prison. It's a prison of the mind where fear of losing control prevails. It's exhausting.

Pre the 'Mark Moment', I had many ways of avoiding honouring these parts of me. Apart from the beauties mentioned above: shaming myself and indulging in it completely, there was one more strong contender: denial.

Positive thinking is one of the most popular forms of denial used today, and you will see it touted all the time. What's wrong with that, you ask? Positive thinking is great when it leads to positive changes in your life, but what about when it stops you from taking positive action and making positive changes? Well, then it becomes a blocker, and then it becomes denial. This bid to be positive is so one-dimensional and ele-mentary. I would stare at myself in a mirror (as the books taught me to do) and tell myself I was amazing, yet deep down, I was unwilling to accept that I was simultaneously com-pletely unamazing.

So, there you are pretending you are certain things and not others, trying to make everything positive rather than feel the sting of truth. I did that for years and I see it now in the people I coach. People get close to embracing the bits they would ra-ther not be, people get close to making the changes they know they need to make, but that feeling comes in, that discomfort takes over, and all of a sudden, there they are, telling them-selves things aren't so bad. It's a protection mechanism, and as is the case with protection mechanisms, they take energy and are only viable for so long.

The other way you can deny the bits of you that you don't like is by projecting them onto the people around you. My dad isn't the most philosophical of men, yet I'll never forget him saying:

"It can't always be everyone else's fault, you know."

(I'm sure if Socrates had said that it'd be all over the internet by now.)

It's incredible how often people bounce from relationship to relationship, job to job or argument to argument, hitting the same obstacles repeatedly without seeing the common denominator (that would be you/me.) It was never my fault. People never understood me, never loved me enough, and they were always assholes. In truth, I needed to honour and see the asshole in me. The fact is that I never understood myself, never loved myself enough and I did not see it was very often my doing that things didn't work out.

Projecting the bits you don't like about yourself onto others isn't something you consciously do, yet you do it. You will give advice to others that you need to take for yourself, and you will see in others what you don't want to see in yourself. It's an excellent way of avoiding the work. After all, if the problem is outside of you, you no longer need to do anything about it. The trouble is, it's a painful way to avoid doing the work because your life begins to follow the same pattern repeatedly until you take the hint.

You may now start to look at life and think: 'It's me. I have been blaming others and projecting all of my shit onto them'. But, before you beat yourself up, remember that everyone does this. Now that you know you do it you can start to notice when you do. At that point, you can reclaim those bits of you that need some work and understanding.

The reality is we *all* struggle with these things. We all struggle to honour the so-called crap bits of us and our lives. Don't beat yourself up for that. If you do, remember that you are human and that creating the perfect mind mansion is not the aim. Having one that is whole and that you get to move around freely in is, but to achieve, you have to build up the courage to look at the rooms you fear going into.

It's not all bad you know...

If there is one thing I know, it's that we are generally great at seeing what's wrong with us (then running from, indulging in or denying it). However, when it comes to seeing how great we are, we are flat out terrible at even acknowledging it.

It's incredible how often people learn to hide the great bits about themselves or simply can't even see how great they are and so, as always, tend to project it all onto others. You will see how confident people are, you will see others' beauty, you will even tell them about it, all the while missing your own beauty and confidence. I remember being at an event where we went around the room telling the people there what we admired about them. It was amazing how, when a person spoke about what they admired in the other people there, you could see that what they had chosen to say was also a quality they had but didn't recognise in themselves. Not honouring and embracing the great and the good bits about yourself will also cause problems, just as much as not honouring the bad.

When you can't see the great bits about yourself, you will tend to feel a void which you rely on others, money, success, or the perfect person who treats you in the perfect way to fill. Of course, none of those things fills the gap you feel. That gap can only be filled by what you are refusing to see and embrace in yourself, all that great, unique stuff which is already there.

The truth is that the great things you see in others, the people you admire, respect, or look up to, you too have the capabilities for these inside of you. Next time you find yourself telling someone how great they are, give yourself the same compliment and see how it feels. It may feel uncomfortable, and if it does, you will undoubtedly know that it's something you are unwilling to see in yourself. Wholeness will come from honouring all of you, and some of you may just find it harder to embrace the 'good' bits than you do the 'bad' bits.

Letting go of what was, to access what could be

It's worth repeating that this chapter of the book has been about accepting and honouring all the parts of who you are so that you can roam your mind mansion freely, no longer in fear of stumbling into a bad room that you cannot get back out of.

It's been my attempt to help you see that trying to force into creation a perfect mind mansion, that you and everyone else agrees on as being good and nice and worthy of exposure, will leave you limited and living in fear of experiencing the totality of your personhood. Reclaiming and integrating all of your disowned parts and making friends with the 'enemy' you have created within will open up a whole load of energy and focus, as well as happiness and peace of mind.

We must next talk about one of the primary reasons that we become scared of the rooms in our mind mansion – our experiences.

You experience something that dramatically changes how you feel, and when that happens you are flung into a room of your mind mansion that you would rather not be in. You feel ways you would rather not feel. You think thoughts you would rather not think. Maybe, you start to take actions that you know aren't really who you want to be.

Over time, the strength of that experience starts to fade and life may return to some kind of normality. However, that experience is lodged away in a room of your mind mansion, charged with energy, pulling your attention in there all the time. At some point, that old experience will get triggered. You bump into the person, visit a similar place, see a similar behaviour, and that experience is once again activated, along with all the feelings and thoughts that come with it.

I call this 'brain junk'. All the stuff lodged away in the rooms of your mind is pulling your focus. You cannot seem to stay away, and your focus pulls away from you. Your mental energy drains, and as you unconsciously work hard to suppress the pull, it triggers you into responses you seem to have no control over.

Yet again, you are faced with the same challenge, i.e. letting go of the energy around it all. Maybe that experience was something you caused, or perhaps it was someone else. It doesn't matter which. It is important to endeavour to let it go anyway and to let go of the energy around that experience.

It would be rash of me, even a little dangerous, to break down techniques to release old, tied-up energy in your system. That sort of thing needs expert guidance. This section is purely here to help you see some ways you can use to *start* to move forward and give you some keys to do that.

United States Army Behavioural Science Officer Stephanie D. Nelson outlined a treatment of individuals who had served in the military and were suffering from PTSD. Her treatment plan includes several techniques that, the evidence suggests, will help those suffering from symptoms of PTSD. The methods used were categorised into four chronological stages of treatment progression:

1. Deal
2. Feel
3. Heal
4. Seal

We have used many of these concepts in our coaching work.

One analogy used in this treatment plan, which I have found useful for people, is to think of the mind as a filing cabinet. A lot of the experiences, that you might look at as brain junk, are files that have become messed up and out of order. They have infiltrated all of your other files and that is how past incidents can tend to bleed into other areas of your life. That incident where you got hurt in a relationship, stops you from trusting in other relationships and shows up in your interactions with people. That incident where you failed and felt stupid, shows up in your job when you get asked to progress, and you refuse because the thought of it projects that experience back into your mind. So, by letting go you are tidying up these files a touch, putting them all into some sort of order and filing things away, for reference yes, but with much less emotional charge attached to them.

One of the most useful ways to start this process is to write about it. Start with the facts of what happened, how it made you feel and what you were thinking. Of course, that brings up lots of emotion. This is not bad. It's simply us getting it out there. From there, you need to start finding some meaning around the topic. This is where the opportunity arises to cultivate a meaning that is now useful for you. You can choose a more powerful and useful meaning to attach to the experience: You can acknowledge how the experience has brought you to where you are. Yes, many of the effects may have been unpleasant. However, within that experience you can find lessons to learn. It may have made you more empathetic, stronger, and more determined. From here, what can you do with this? You can't change the past. However, you can choose how the story finishes.

We all carry brain junk around. We all hold onto things that have shaped how we see ourselves and others in ways that don't help us. The thing to remember is that it's never too late to let go of them and that letting go will allow you to build a future that no longer repeats the same old patterns. It will allow you to move around your mind mansion with a sense of freedom. Past experiences will still be there, yet no longer charged with the emotion that triggers you into responses that keep you stuck. Create the most powerful meaning for yourself moving forward, learn the lessons, express the emotions attached and start to build the future you desire, not the one you are trying to avoid.

A great place to start with this process is to pick a room of your mind mansion you would rather not spend so much time in. Maybe it's worry, stress, anger, or sadness. Simply pick a room that you feel is a chronic issue. There will undoubtedly be an incident that caused you to get thrown in there, but you don't have to get that deep. You can start by writing about that room, how it makes you feel, what it makes you think and what it makes you do when you are there. You can follow the same process from there: pulling lessons from it all, finding new meaning, and finally choosing how the story ends.

It may seem simplistic or even silly to process the energy around how you feel, but one of the things that robs you of your mental freedom is how you feel about certain rooms in that mind mansion of yours. Most people identify with these feelings so strongly that they become who they believe they are: 'an anxious person; 'an angry person', 'an overthinker.'

Getting it all out and choosing a new narrative can be one of the most powerful things you can do. These rooms can no longer define you. They are things you experience, not who you are. You can let go of the energy around those beliefs.

Try this

It's time to put some of this into practice. The following steps are straightforward ways to start honouring some of the rooms in your mind mansion you might be afraid of and seeing and acknowledging your strengths.

You will need a pen and paper and a bit of peace and quiet.

Step 1: Honour the dark

A. Write down some of the traits you'd rather not have.

B. Ask yourself if, used healthily, they could actually help you or others.

C. Write as many ways as you can think of, how each one could be used positively.

If this is tricky, think about a scaled-back version of the quality.

Step 2: Find your light

A. Write down three people you admire

B. Write down three qualities you admire in each person.

C. Go through the list of qualities and find at least one time you have displayed each quality.

Congratulations, you just reclaimed some of your great bits!

Step 3: Accept yourself

A. Set a timer for five minutes

B. Close your eyes and go back to breathing how you have been taught to, throughout this book.

C. On every few breaths out say "I appreciate myself".

D. Pay attention to how that feels.

E. Now, on every few breaths out say "I accept myself"

F. Pay attention to how that feels.

G. Now, on every few breaths out say "I love myself"

H. Pay attention to how that feels.

I. Now, on every few breaths out say "I forgive myself"

J. Pay attention to how that feels.

A quick recap

The key to having a free mind and good levels of focus starts with making friends with your mind. Seek to understand the rooms of your mind mansion and recognise the ones you are trying to destroy or avoid.

1. Become aware of how you indulge the so-called bad rooms of your mind mansion through self-pity or the take me as I am approach. Seek to honour them instead.

2. Positive thinking is helpful, until it turns into denial and stops you from taking positive action.

3. Projection is another way you will avoid seeing certain things about yourself. You will project advice onto others that could benefit you, as well as the bits of you that you would rather not be. You will also recognise positive traits in others that you fail to see that you also possess.

4. A significant reason you become afraid of certain rooms of your mind mansion is previous experience. These previous experiences cause brain junk that affects how you see yourself and your world. Reducing the charge around them will free up lots of mental focus.

8

SKIPPING STEPS AND CHEATING TIME

You can't skip steps, and you can't cheat time. It's tempting, after all, to want to speed the process up and get to where you want faster. But it's important to note there are steps you simply cannot skip. I want to share things that will ensure you take the information and steps laid out here and transfer them into practical action. After all, unless you do something practical with this advice, you won't see any of the benefits you have read about.

There are three fundamentals want to encourage you to build on and three steps that will be crucial to take. It's important you do them in order. Progress is important, but at the right pace. You can't skip these steps without some kind of kickback, which usually means falling back to where you started.

Build awareness

We are overwhelmed with calls to raise awareness these days, yet that's not really what I am talking about here.

The first key to making changes is to become aware of yourself, where you are in life, and where you want to be. What's working for you and what isn't. Your strengths, weaknesses, gifts, and flaws. Your limitations and your possibilities.

When you become aware of these things, you can start to do something with them. Very often, you will focus your awareness on where you are and how bad you feel that is. As you read in Part 1 of this book, you must become aware of what you want and where you are going. Very often, you are unaware of the life you have or could have, and even less aware of the stuff holding you back. Now you have a raised awareness of many things that will help you move forward.

Build skills

Being aware of what needs changing and ways to change it is great. The only trouble is that awareness alone is not going to transform your life. Knowing what to do is very different to doing what you know. Skills are the answer.

It's easy to fall into the trap of thinking that learning is the same as building skills. It isn't. That is why this book is loaded with steps to take at the end each chapter Take everything you have learnt and make it practical, because what you know isn't going to calm you down, get you clear, help you escape burnout or up your focus, but what you 'do' is.

Skills take practice and time to develop. Build your skills, and you will be confident in dealing with what life throws your way and building the life you want and the challenges that come with that. Skills really are the gap between where you are now and where you want to be.

Build a life

What's the point of all these skills if you don't use them to improve your life? It's easy to get caught up on the personal development train, stopping and picking up courses, skills, and hacks and then not actually changing the things you want to change in life. Set a vision of what you want your life to be like and work on building that. Change what you can, accept what you can't and create what you want.

It's tempting to jump straight in after reading some inspirational words and decide to overhaul your life, right now. You might make rash decisions and regret after it, skipping the steps of building solid awareness and the skills to help you. The best-case scenario is you fall off the wagon by midweek and keep stopping and starting. The worst-case scenario is you jump in and make terrible life decisions that are hard to reverse, on the high of some random inspirational insight that was completely dopamine-fuelled, and excitement driven, but with no real thought about possible consequences.

The moral of the tale here is simple. Don't stay just being aware of what's possible or what needs changing and don't think reading this book is enough to transform your life because it isn't. Seek to build practical skills and then look towards changing the things that need changing in your life. Cheating time or skipping these steps often looks like it's the fastest route to what you want. In my experience though, it's always the slowest in the long term.

Yes, change is hard. At the time of writing, I have just been having video calls with our academy graduates. Their stories of transformation are amazing, but not one left our call without telling me how it got really hard at times. Every one of them had hit real sticking points because changing things *is* hard. The flip side of that is that keeping things the same is also hard.

Getting fit and healthy is hard, yet so is being unfit and unhealthy. Building a business is hard, yet so is doing something that you hate each day to make a living. Building a solid relationship is hard, yet so is having an unhappy one. You get the picture; it's all hard. There is a difference between these two kinds of hard, though.

The stress that comes with tolerating a life you don't want is the kind of hard that breaks you down, and you become weaker for it. You lose confidence, motivation, desire, and your spark, because it takes hard work and effort to deal with the things you don't want. It takes effort to plaster over the cracks of what isn't working for you, and it takes time and energy to tolerate a mind and body that isn't serving you at all. Time and energy could be switched into working towards improving all of that.

On the other hand, the type of stress that comes with making an effort to build the life you want is the type of hard work that builds you up. You become stronger for it as your confidence, self-esteem and everything else grows. Sure, you will hit obstacles and setbacks along the way, but solving these problems is fulfilling and will make you much stronger and more capable.

This kind of hard rewards you with more energy, enthusiasm, and drive. It's the kind of hard that just doesn't feel as hard.

So yes, change is going to be hard, but you are used to that already. When you choose to make the changes you want to, you are choosing the kind of hard that fulfils you and helps you grow as a person. This impacts not only your life but the lives of those around you in the most positive of ways.

It really does matter

When making changes feels like it's getting hard, you will justify your way out of doing the work in many ways. You will forget its importance, and that is perfectly natural. Just like when you feel fear and try to escape that, you will do the same when things get hard on your journey. Don't beat yourself up for that; become aware of it and adjust accordingly.

You may become the magical thinker who convinces yourself that there will be a better time in the future to do the work, and that you will get used to this current state of affairs. Magical thinkers invent an 'easier' future to avoid the reality of what needs to be done today.

On the other hand, denial thinkers take the now and make it 'not so bad' when things get hard, so they no longer have to take action. Positivity is a funny thing. It can easily become a reason not to act on what we want, rather than the fuel to do what we know will help us. If you are happy doing that, then crack on. Bear in mind, if you find yourself constantly looking to change things and then finding reasons to convince yourself that now is actually ok after all and nothing needs to change, you are probably using some form of denial thinking.

Or lastly, maybe you start to fall into 'need to know' thinking, where you need to know that everything is going to work before you even try to change what you want. You look at the future and refuse to act until you know it will work out. You need proof and evidence that it will all be OK. The reality is no one knows what the future will hold. Sure, you can have a rough idea based on past experience and evidence, but no one knows for sure. The interesting thing here is that when you get into a need-to-know mind-set, no amount of evidence or reassurance seems enough, and yet again you convince yourself that maybe it doesn't matter at all.

All these thinking patterns allow you to avoid the hard work that comes with moving forward. Instead, they lead you back to the things you weren't happy with in the first place. Notice it happening and remind yourself that if what you want didn't matter, you wouldn't keep coming back to it time after time.

There is a path, after all

Based on all my time coaching, I can bring change down to three solid progressions that need to be made. Each comes with its own set of problems and pitfalls that will sometimes crop up and cause you to fall back to the start. You can't skip stages as that will bite you in the arse down the line.

The foundation

Building a solid foundation is the crucial first step to being greater than your current reality. This stage could be called getting your house in order. When you lay the building blocks correctly and consistently, you stay the course and achieve the changes you want. It is about creating some decent solid pillars: the vision, energy and focus pillars; and getting those basics set in stone in your life. No one is perfect, you will miss days and fall off, but the intention to nail those basics consistently is the aim at first.

This, too, comes with problems. The first problem is that you will try and move too fast. You will end up rushing through this step, and before you know it, your attention isn't focused on getting your own house in order; it's on everyone else in your life. It is on the fact your goals aren't coming quickly enough and it is on helping others. The trouble is your foundation isn't strong enough to support that, so you crash, burn and fall straight back to the start. Becoming aware of those patterns is crucial. Notice and adjust your focus back to handling yourself. Becoming behaviour focussed over goal focussed will help you a lot.

Another common problem is settling at 'coping'. You may be tempted just to settle here. After all, you were struggling before, and now you find you are coping. So, you start to settle. The trouble is coping is exhausting. And you guessed it, we fall back to struggling. You can get pretty good at this, and before you know it, you can bounce from struggling to coping until you burn out and get fed up. Noticing your tendency to stop at OK is key.

Notice and remind yourself that if you keep pushing on with progressing your foundation, you will move past coping, and unless life lifes, you will never go back to chronically struggling again.

The lighthouse

When you have your foundation in order as well as you can, and you feel like you are no longer struggling daily, you are starting to feel like you are in a great place; moving to stage two is a must. This is where we begin to think about the other people in our life. As mentioned, connecting with others is vital to our well-being and happiness.

Of all the stages I have observed, this one has the most dangers. When you change, it can be difficult for other people and it can also be difficult for you. You can feel like you don't fit in. Maybe your preferences change and you feel a little out of place. It's common, and it can blow up in your face when you don't know how to handle it.

This can often show up as you trying to change everyone around you and becoming the tugboat we spoke about earlier. You cause yourself to burn out or, even worse, push the people you care about away from you. Very often, when you find you can't change people you will start removing them. Too many relationships fall apart unnecessarily at this point because you haven't yet found peace in allowing people to be who they are while at the same time being comfortable with who you are.

Lastly, and sadly a common one, you will find it easier to go back to old ways so you can feel like you fit in again. A vital step in all personal progression is to connect with others. If you can't do that after you have connected with yourself you will fall apart, and as explained above, if you try and do it in ways that aren't useful, it will blow up in your face. This is where you need to become the lighthouse discussed in Chapter 3. This will help you with this stage of your progression.

Mastery

Once you have passed through the stage of being a lighthouse, the final stage of progression is often the hardest but the most fun. It's the point where, if you pass through it, this new way of being that you have created is second nature. It no longer feels like an effort to think, feel or be this way. You have changed at the core of who you are, and your identity has morphed. Gone are the words 'I am just an anxious person' or whatever you used to define yourself as. Gone are the 'This is just the way I am' phrases after each setback or cock up. You see yourself differently, and you see the world differently. The crazy thing is you aren't a different person at all. You are just the real you, that you always knew was there somewhere. There is no more 'old me' that you keep chained up and afraid. In the mastery stage, you have embraced yourself, undoubtedly forgiven yourself and found peace in who you are whilst still following your desire to do greater things.

You will know you have reached mastery when it feels like there is nothing to hide or prove to others or yourself anymore. Don't mistake this for "I may as well stop here". I have seen so many people sabotage themselves at this point. Rather than thinking the better it gets, the better it can get, you give up and fail to see that you can feel even greater depths of well-being in your life. Having nothing to prove doesn't mean you are no longer pursuing your desires for your life, just because the game is at an end. It means you are now playing the game simply because you enjoy playing it; you wouldn't have it any other way. Your goals are inspiring and feel great to pursue, yet at the same time, you know life is great without them.

Having nothing to hide doesn't mean you have destroyed all the elements of you that you would rather not be. It means you have integrated them, made peace with them, and you are back to being whole. When you get stuck here, going back to chapter 7, Making Friends with the Enemy, will help you navigate this stage with skill and grace.

I firmly believe that you don't have to keep guessing. You can follow a path lit up in front of you, and that path can take you wherever you want. Ultimately, we are all individuals, but the approach, initially, is the same for everyone. This book follows a simplified and broad path, and the intention is to provide you with the simplest way to get started and keep going.

Throughout all the stages of your journey, you can return to the relevant chapters in this book. You can turn to it for reminders and guidance. I've lost count of how many books I have re-read, a year later, that have hit me differently the second time. It is my aim that this book will be a companion throughout your journey. Something you can pick up and refer back to when you feel stuck, or resistance arises.

And finally, you will forget to do what you know you should be doing. You will make mistakes and forget about this book altogether. But much like the path to change, it will always be here waiting for you to jump back in again. Never convince yourself it's too late, that you are too far gone or that you have been off the path for too long to get back on.

You can always start again with the next decision you make. You can start again and remember this; you are never starting from scratch; you always have the great habits and choices of your past sitting there. So, keep up the good work. Give yourself a break, and always remember that change requires you to be slightly less shit than you were yesterday.

A quick recap

Change is challenging but vital. Take things step by step. Start by understanding yourself, then proceed to developing your skills and strategy. Shape improvements to fit your life. Always remember, it's worth the effort.

1. Making change is hard; it is common to want to speed up the process and skip steps. However, it is important to take your time and take the practical steps provided in this book at the right time and in the right order.

2. Building self-awareness is crucial.

3. Building skills comes next, and along with self-awareness, these two aspects of change are important drivers towards building a life....

4. Building a life. It is important to improve your life in a way that is individual to *you*, using the self-awareness and the skills you have learned. Seek to build practical skills and then look towards changing the things that need changing in your life.

5. Change is hard, but so is tolerating a life that you don't want.

CHANGE
EXPERIENCES

Discover how other people felt
when they decided to change...

Derek

"The feedback I got from family and friends was so humbling to hear... had me in tears if I'm honest... telling me that I'm an inspiration to them, a good honest and genuine person and to keep being me..."

"(Friends and family) said they're glad to see me back to my old self, happier and better equipped to deal with what life throws at me...."

Lynda

"I signed up to Unbreakable because I had completely lost my way. I had postnatal depression, I had lost both my parents and had stopped even doing the basics like looking after myself. I wasn't living. I was barely surviving. Now, I am in control and am fully responsible for my life and my happiness. Some key things are:

- I wake up happy most days
- I don't allow others' judgements to affect me
- I believe in myself
- I allow myself to feel all emotions
- I celebrate my wins
- I have better self confidence
- I have better relationships with family and friends
- I have the skills to deal with whatever life throws at me
- I don't allow difficult issues to drag out and affect me for days, or weeks on end
- I am off all antidepressants

Aneta

When I decided to change, I was at my breaking point. I was in survival mode, burned out, low on energy, with horrible back pain, with unprocessed grief and not taking phone calls. I felt helpless seeing my kids suffering mentally due to lockdowns.... Then, I decided to fully commit to myself and give myself one of my best birthday presents and change my life. How do I feel now? Huge improvement! Where do I start?

- I am happy
- I have more energy and I do not need coffee to stay awake
- My back pain is gone
- I learnt how to create boundaries
- My kids are happy
- I became more confident
- I invest in myself, in my hobbies
- I do not need others' acceptance to feel good
- I processed lots of negative emotions and I am now more calm and mindful.
- An obstacle is no longer a problem but an opportunity to learn
- I have more friends, my community is growing

Chris

I used to depend on my medication for my anxiety for the last five years, but three months off them and I have started to be able to deal with stress and find solutions to my problems much easier and calmer. I now have the tools to start feeling more focussed and I am a much nicer person to be around!

I react differently to stressful situations, which do still happen. Even my wife said she's amazed with how calmer and driven I am in creating a better future for all the family.

Les

"I no longer struggle with anxiety, I have ways of managing it now. If I have intrusive thoughts, I don't analyse them or dwell on them, I just move on and get on with my day. I have developed more positive beliefs about myself and life in general and I have better relationships with people. I was able to return to work after seven months of sick leave. Things I find easier:

- Getting outside more
- Exercising
- Making new friends
- Going to work
- Going into crowded areas
- Challenging my negative beliefs
- Setting new goals

I am proud that I have come through all these things and I was able to return to work and see a way to get back on with my life. I am also proud that I have better insight into how the mind works and I have greater self-awareness when I find myself slipping back into my old ways.

Ally

I was feeling burnt out, an emotional wreck not knowing what to do with my emotions. I kept mulling over past traumas and hurts... I felt angry all the time. My days felt like I was in groundhog day doing the same thing over and over with no time for myself and I was snapping and grumpy. I knew I didn't want to feel like that but I didn't know how not to.

Now I'm finding it easier to get up and be focused on the day ahead. I am most proud of myself, still having a bit of anxiety going out, but I do my breathing and focus so that I now have an 'I can do this' attitude. I'm more energetic and calmer in stressful situations. I feel that my communication to others is better than before and my attitude is more forgiving. I am not letting the past bother me so much. It's been and gone and I can move forward. I love the saying: 'be the lighthouse and not the tugboat,' and I love the mind mansion.

KEEP IN TOUCH

Everything you need to get started and see progress in your life is in this book. I genuinely believe that. However, I also know some people prefer additional help, quicker results, and comprehensive support. If that sounds like you, follow this link to join our community enjoying the 'Unbreakable Reboot'. I'd love to see you there.

- unbreakablereboot.com/reboot

You can also send me a message using this link:

- m.me/SimonUnbreakable

There's also a free Facebook group where you can meet with like-minded people, if you would like:

- facebook.com/SimonUnbreakable

Best wishes,

Simon

NOTES

NOTES

NOTES

Printed in Great Britain
by Amazon

38297811R00096